"Our family has been very blessed by the fact that God decided to keep Joe Cooper around. Joe's love of kids and sports have led him to be a faithful supporter and attendant of many different sports events for all three of our kids. My kids know they are loved and feel very special because of Joe. He is a wonderful, generous Christian man!"

John and Ellen Calipari,
University of Memphis Basketball Coach

"As Scoutmaster with Boy Scout Troop 75, I have personally had the pleasure of getting to know Mr. Cooper. Mr. Cooper's time as a Scout, as revealed in this text, reflects the timeless values the Scouting program instills in young men of the past, present, and future."

Steven A. Williamson

jesus
MY HERO

jesus
MY HERO

JOSEPH M. COOPER SR.

TATE PUBLISHING & Enterprises

Published by Tate Publishing & Enterprises, LLC
127 E. Trade Center Terrace | Mustang, Oklahoma 73064 USA
1.888.361.9473 | www.tatepublishing.com

Tate Publishing is committed to excellence in the publishing industry. The company reflects the philosophy established by the founders, based on Psalm 68:11,
"The Lord gave the word and great was the company of those who published it."

Book design copyright © 2008 by Tate Publishing, LLC. All rights reserved.
Cover design by Steven Jeffrey
Interior design by Stephanie Woloszyn

Published in the United States of America

ISBN: 978-1-60462-943-9
1. Christian Living: Practical Life
08.05.05

This is the life story of Joe Cooper who went from being a loving and obedient child, to a rebellious teenager, to a self-serving young adult, to a notorious sinner; from a rowdy, drunken sinner, to a born again Christian; through misunderstanding his father, two failed marriages, a massive heart attack, and heart transplant to a servant of Christ.

This book is not written to bring honor to Joe Cooper or anyone who is mentioned in it, but to bring honor to God the Father, Jesus the Son, and the Holy Spirit.

"Therefore, go and make disciples of all nations, baptizing them in the name of the Father, and the Son, and the Holy Spirit."

Matthew 28:19

Thank you, my God, my Father for the donor of this heart. This extended life of mine and this book are dedicated to the donor, who is unknown to me, and the family who exemplified Your love as taught by Jesus.

"And you must love others as much as you love yourself."

Mark 12:31

INTRODUCTION

Stay on the Jesus Road.
All others lead to heartache and pain.

Psalm 25:4 "Show me the path where I should walk, O Lord; point out the right road for me to follow."

Proverbs 12:28 "The way of the godly leads to life; their path does not lead to death."

Proverbs 14:2 "Those who follow the right path fear the Lord; those who take the wrong path despise him."

Isaiah 6:8 "Then I heard the Lord asking, 'Whom should I send as a messenger to my people? Who will go for us?' And I said, 'Lord, I'll go; send me.'"

In each life, there are so many decisions, What must I do? What is right? Which way should I go? There are forks in the road of life. Ask not, what is easiest or more enjoyable, but what would Jesus do.

Joe Cooper

THE JESUS ROAD

Heart Transplant

My commitment of this new heart is to my God and His Son, Jesus Christ, the Creator and Master of all the universe with whom nothing is impossible.

> "And we know that God causes everything to work together for those who love God and are called according to His purpose for them."
>
> Romans 8:28

My dear Father God, I commit and surrender this new heart to your service. Please, in the name of Jesus, let me keep this heart clean, pure, kind, generous, thoughtful, and as a Christian example at all times. Please don't let me ever stain it with any intentional sin as I did the heart that you gave me at birth.

Let me carry out whatever the plan is for the remainder of this life that you have for me. Give me the courage, wisdom, and strength to glorify you, Father; your Son,

Jesus; and the Holy Spirit into any task or situation you may give me. I know that you, in me, can do anything.

"Commit everything you do to the Lord. Trust Him and He will help you."

Psalms 37:5

Monday, June 7, 2004, 9 a.m.

My Godsend, Patricia, my wife, checked me into Baptist Memorial Hospital in Memphis, Tennessee. The circumstances were that I would be in the heart unit until either I pass away from this life and go to Jesus, or have a heart transplant. I had just turned sixty-five in April and had suffered with congestive heart failure for eight years. On February 26, 1996, I suffered major damage from a heart attack. Dr. Eric Johnson and his wonderful staff from the Stern Cardiovascular Clinic had been taking care of me for these eight years. A man of tremendous faith who my family and I love as a brother in Christ, Dr. Johnson has shared the wisdom and talents bestowed upon him by God to keep me alive to this day. Thank you, my friend, and thanks to your wife and son.

"Blessed is the man who reveres God."

Proverbs 28:14

Monday evening, June 7, 2004, 6 p.m.

My oldest child, Joseph M. Cooper, Jr., "Mike," was at the hospital with me, as was Patricia. Dr. Johnson came in to visit, and he brought me up to date on my condition and the plan to treat it. Dr. Ed Garret joined us.

Dr. Garrett was the surgeon in charge of the transplant center. He told the nurse to keep anyone else out of my room, as he wanted a private visit with just those there. They told me that I only had a short time to live with my condition, and a heart transplant was the only thing left to do. I told them that this was okay. I came into this to battle until the end. We all agreed and there were smiles on every face and several amens. Doctors Garrett and Johnson then told us that if everything was ready, they would move me to the Transplant Isolation Unit on Tuesday, June 8, 2004.

Tuesday evening, June 8, 2004

The nurses came to take me to the Isolated Transplant Unit. Upon arrival, I was met by Eric and Dean, two of the finest young men you would ever want to meet. They were my RNs for the night.

Let me take the time to tell about this heart transplant unit and the medical people who work here. This may be the most efficient and compassionate group of individuals on Planet Earth. To the last one, they will share scripture, pray, and tell about their salvation with you.

"Joy fills hearts that are planning for good."
Proverbs 12:20

These people should have a training film made for the medical and nursing schools to use in the classroom. My caregivers were Eric, Dean, Brian, Shannon, Ed, Jim, Anthony, Bill, Stacey, Lillian, Tracy, Amy, Lindsey, Stacy, Magnolia, Eunice, Betty, and Catherine, my lady from the Nutrition Center who helped with my meals. To anyone that I may have forgotten, I thank my God for you. May He bless and keep you always.

Eric and Brian told me room 2939 would be my home for who knew how long. They wheeled me into my new shiny, spotless room, which was the most equipped hospital room I had ever seen. The IV stand was equipped with four dispensers and monitors. Another stand was equipped with a separate monitor. On the other side of the bed was another monitor to continuously account my blood pressure, heart rate, oxygen level, etc. Then, there was the oxygen that I would be on as long as long as I was there. These two young men got me into my bed and went to work hooking me up to all this equipment. They were very efficient and friendly. It didn't take them long.

I was confined to a space of about twelve feet for how long, only God knew.

"Be glad for all God is planning for you, be patient in trouble and prayerful always."

Romans 12:12

June 8, 2004, 11 *p.m.*

All settled in and off to Dreamland. For the next eighteen days I was hooked up to multiple IVs as the doctors were getting me ready for a heart transplant.

There were so many medications to prepare the body for a new organ.

These were the people who came to visit me before the transplant: my minister, Dr. Steve Shapard; my dear mother (more about her later); Susan, my sister, and her husband, Bob Wilson; Patricia and her children came daily. Shelley flew in twice from her home in Panama City, Florida, for several days.

My first visitors: Germantown High School softball girls, for I was their substitute granddad and spiritual advisor, Christian counselor, confidant, and friend to the children and parents of all I come in contact with.

> "Jesus told them, you are to go into the world and preach the good news to everyone, everywhere. Those who believe and are baptized will be saved, but those who refuse to believe will be condemned."
>
> Mark 16:15-16

Others who visited were John Bramlett (more about him later); J.W. and Gloria Adams; Red Palmer; Terry Austin; Beau Martin (who brought me the signed baseball from his first high school win as a pitcher); Beau's parents, Gerald and Connie Martin; sister, Katie (softball player); Betty Hayes and daughter, Brittany (softball); Lynn and Toni Gast (another softball player); Rick and Stacey Berry and their two sons, Zach and Eli, who brought a banner for my room—what a fine young family; Richard Robison (more later); Don Lewis; Betty Wright; my golfing group "The Hallelujah Hackers" (more later); Bobby and Pam Armbruister and Michelle; David and Suzie Laramie; Charlie White, coach of the Germantown High School 5A state champions; Ken Netherland, retired GHS coach and a legend in high school football as the winning-est coach in Shelby County history and named in the High School Hall of Fame (USA); Ernest Chism, retired principal GHS for more than thirty years and now a member of the county school board and candidate for city alderman; Skip Brewer; Jerry Ellis; Dean Gordon; my nephew, Troy Matthews, who is like another son to me; Shannon Cook; Sette Brucker; Rick Hale; Richard "Casper" Hillhouse; Jim Angel; Jim Loosier; Jan Long; Betty Loosier; Bob Rose; Russ Vollmer; Bob Freudiger and Jim Whitmire, who are ministers of music at Bellevue Baptist Church in Memphis. (Jim is internationally known for directing one of the largest Christian choirs in existence and his production of Christmas and Easter Passion plays—a dedicated man of God); Lindsey Martin, a beautiful young lady who is like another grandchild; Lamar, Almedia and Natia Shores, dear friends and like family; Coach John Calipari, University of Memphis, and his wife, Ellen, a faithful Christian family in service, attendance, love, and example who have three super children, Erin, Megan, and Bradley a.k.a. Hardhead; Coach Cal, who had heard I was in the transplant unit at church on Sunday, June 12. He was just three weeks from having hip replacement surgery. That afternoon, on two crutches, he and Ellen were there to see me.

"But the good man walks along in the ever brightening light of God's favor."

Proverbs 5:18

As the days passed, I moved up on the national recipient list from third to first. Oh, did I mention that my blood type, O negative, is not interchangeable with any other? I need a large (200 lbs.+) O negative donor. This was the category that I had reached first in.

Early in the evening Saturday, June 26, 2004

I was watching TV and doing a crossword puzzle. Chandra, the transplant coordinator, stuck her head in the door to see how I was doing. She was wearing her operating room cover and told me that she had come to get the lady down the hall because they had a heart for her. I was so happy for this person that I hollered, "Amen!" Chandra then shocked me. She said that when they were finished with her, she was coming back for me. I almost fainted. I screamed. I hugged her. The other nurses were cheering, "God is good, all the time." Then they all left me alone for a few minutes, and I prayed, "*Father God, please be with the family of my heart donor, and thank you, Jesus, for loving me.*"

My family started arriving: Mom, Susan and Bob, Patricia, Halle and Michael, and John "Bull" Bramlett; also Rich Hale, Brian's friend, and Carrie Cannon, Halle's friend. Darren and Shelly, my other two children, were out of town or working. The nurses began shaving me all over and wiping me down with disinfectant. I was so clean.

Saturday, June 26, 2004, 11 p.m.

They came to take me to surgery. With everyone by my side, "Bull" Bramlett prayed. I just kept saying, "Thank you, Jesus." Chandra, the coordinator, Shannon and Brian, RNs, wheeled me to the operating room.

> "O Lord, hear me as I pray, pay attention to my groaning."
>
> Psalms 5:1

Baby Joe, 1939   Mama (Marguerite)

Dr. Ed Garrett and his transplant team were ready. I was put upon the operating table and cleaned one more

time. Well, this was it. I would either have a successful transplant or the alternative—rejection or possibly
death. But the peace of God was with me and I prayed,
"Father, Thy will be done." The anesthesiologist gave me
theee———out!

Back about Sixty Years: 1941

Jonas Ridge is a village high in the Blue Ridge Mountains of
western North Carolina. When I was a two-year-old tow-
head, I stayed with my grandparents, Lloyd, Sr. and Tuppy
Barrier. My mom, Marguerite, was teaching school away
and could only get home about once a month. Bill, Libby,
Katie, and Jo Ann, my uncle and aunts, were still living at
home and attending high school. My granddad owned the
Country Grocery and he had several other interests, such
as shrubbery and lumber. I went to the store and hung out
with Paw and all the folks who came to the store.

1942

Paw got sick with a stomach ulcer and the doctors couldn't
fix him. He died. They brought his body home for visitation, as was the custom then. That was the first time
I remember crying. Tuppy Weatherman Barrier "Maw"
was still a legend in the mountains of western North
Carolina. She was a Christian in every meaning: trust-
worthy, moral, kind, caring, giving, sharing, lodged the
homeless, fed the hungry. Families still tell of her helping
their parents or grandparents in times of need.

"If you must choose, take a good name rather than great riches; for to be held in loving esteem is better than silver and gold."

Proverbs 22:1

Tuppy Barrier Family

Family Cabin

Outhouse

After Paw passed away, Libby married my new uncle, John Smith, from over in Pineola, North Carolina, about four miles away. Katie soon married Howard Woodie from Jonas Ridge. JoAnn went to Berea, Kentucky, to college. Uncle Bill went away to the army. Then it was just Maw and me. What a wonderful grandmother. If God were to let me choose, I would have taken the one he gave me—my Maw.

Sometime shortly after, the store burned to the ground. Maw just buckled down and went to raising all of our vegetables, chickens, cows, etc. By then, I was about four years old. Maw taught me to pick the vegetables and bring in kindling wood for the stoves. Our cooking and heat was wood and coal stoves.

Two of the local young men, brothers Ray and Odie Woodie, did the plowing and got Maw's fields ready for planting. Maw was like a mother to them. Like everyone else, they referred to her as "Aunt Tuppy." I was always underfoot with these two, but they liked it.

My best friend was Johnny Ray Barrier, my cousin. Johnny was a couple of years older than me, but we were real pals. There were mountains to climb, caves to explore, trails to hike through the woods, trout fishing in the icy cold streams. Uncle Howard took us on these ventures. (Thanks, Unk! That's what we called him.) Except for Uncle Bill coming home from the army, everything was about the same for the next couple of years. During these first years, my Maw was laying a Christian foundation for me. I still remember walking from our house up the drive and gravel road to Jonas Ridge Methodist Church. It sat about 200 feet higher than the house and was one fourth mile away. It is still there today, having been maintained to perfection, and is still used for every type of Christian service. You can see the church from Maw's front yard. Maw read the Bible to me, told me Bible stories, and did her best to teach me about Jesus.

> "Jesus said, Let the little children come to me, and don't prevent them. For of such is the kingdom of heaven."
>
> Matthew 19:14

My Maw understood this. Thank God for her!

1945

I started Jonas Ridge Elementary School. What a shock! I had to sit still, spell my name, and learn numbers. The one good part was that my Great Aunt Mary Barrier was my teacher. The first grade went okay after all.

Sometime in the fall of 1945, my dad, Harold Cooper, a navy commander, was shipped back to the Norfolk, Virginia Naval Port. Mom had gone to Norfolk earlier and was teaching school and waiting on his return.

They came to Maw's around Christmas 1945, and brought me a shiny new bike, full size—no training wheels! Every pretty day, Johnny Ray and I tried to wear the tires off that bike.

Johnny Ray Barrier still lives in Jonas Ridge, North Carolina, and is married to Betty. He is the father of Jennifer and Cindy and granddad to Evan and Clint. He and Betty founded the Jonas Ridge Assisted Living Home many years ago and still operate it today.

"Do unto others as you would have them do unto you."
Matthew 7:12

June 1, 1946

Maw told me that Mom and Dad were coming to see us. Dad was now off active duty in USN. Mom had left her teaching job in Norfolk. What Maw did not tell me was that Mom and Dad were coming to get me, and we were moving to Jackson, Tennessee. Leaving my grandmother is still a memory I wish I would have never experienced. I can still remember looking out the back window of the car and crying as Maw and Johnnie Ray waved good-bye.

As a six-year-old, I was confused. Would I see my grand-maw and friend again?

> "Trust in the Lord God always, for in the Lord Jehovah
> is your strength."
>
> Isaiah 26:4

The drive to Jackson is about 400 miles, and I got to see things I'd never seen: Burma Shave road signs, "See Rock City" painted on barn roofs, and lots of people. Remember, I had lived in Jonas Ridge, population of 150. On we traveled through Chattanooga and Nashville to Jackson.

Dad had rented one side of a duplex on South Royal Street, not far from the fairgrounds. This was where we would live for the next two months. Dad worked for TVA and was building the electrical power stations around the Jackson area. Mom was pregnant and we went to the park a lot for me to meet kids and play.

July 13, 1946

> "I knew you before I formed you in your mother's
> womb."
>
> Jeremiah 1:5

On this day, the Lord blessed my family and especially me. My sister, Susan, was born. I can remember being so happy until she started crying. Could that baby girl scream! But when I held her, she would get real quiet and look at me with the biggest brown eyes. Those eyes reminded me of the black-eyed susans that grow wild in the Blue Ridge. I have a saying about Susan: "If God had let me choose from all the girls to pick from, I would still until this day, pick the one He gave me." Thank you, God, for Susan. Mom and Susan did well, and both were healthy and happy.

Around the fifteenth of August, we left Jackson and moved to Memphis, arriving in Memphis on a Saturday. Dad, with the help of some local contacts, my great uncle Henry Bagwell and others, had found us a house at 1659 Shadowlawn in South Memphis. It was a nice little brick house in a great neighborhood. There were fourteen or fifteen boys living on the block where our house was, along with several girls. I was soon being initiated into the neighborhood. They all ganged up on me to see if I could take the jokes and tricks they played. It was not long until I was one of them.

> "Praise the Lord, I tell myself, and never forget the good things he does for me."
>
> Psalms 103:2

Only those who were fortunate enough to have been raised in South Memphis will ever know the closeness of all of its people and how we remained friends and supporters of each other until death. There was a loyalty to one another that went far beyond the normal.

Mom and Dad's search for a church home took us to Parkway Methodist, which was about one mile from our house. It was a small, very friendly church, and my

Sunday school teacher was Mrs. Crumpler, a small lady, but one to whom you paid attention. We would continue to attend Parkway Methodist for the next thirteen years.

September, 1946

It was time to enroll me in school. The local elementary school was A. B. Hill, a part of the city school system and about a mile from home. Having done the first grade at Jonas Ridge, I was put in Mrs. Wade's second grade class. Mrs. Wade was a patient but demanding teacher who very quickly got my attention. She demanded that I do good work.

> "And so, My Children, listen to Me. For happy are all who follow My ways."
>
> Proverbs 8:32

At this point, I had a home, church, and school: the three basic things for a neighborhood. Life in Memphis was getting off to a pretty good start. The boys in the neighborhood were always outside playing football in a vacant lot at Shadowlawn and Dison streets, getting up a game of baseball in the street using manhole covers for bases, using tin cans to play kick the can, a game of keep away, or some other physical game.

All the boys on Shadowlawn started the Shadowlawn Pirates, a baseball team to play on neighboring streets. Gordon Stamper, Barry Bright, Roy Szekely, Mike Wallace, Arthur Andrews, Bobby Ginnaven, Billy Borer, Ray Venezie, Artie Clark, and Joe Cooper were the Pirates. No uniforms, just jeans, t-shirts, and tennis shoes (pronounced "tennishoes"), and a glove. Was that ever great fun for a bunch of six- to nine-year-olds!

Sister Susan was growing, walking, talking, and still screaming. Mom and Dad were busy making a living and giving us a home.

Troop 57

Spring 1949

Mr. Caldwell, a member of Parkway Methodist Church and a friend of my dad's, was coaching a junior league baseball team. National Ross Bedding, owned by Mr. Patton, was the sponsor. Mr. Caldwell asked me to try out for the team. I went to the practices and made the team. I was now ten years old and the youngest player on the team. Mr. Caldwell put me at second base. We didn't win many games that year, but we sure had a lot of fun. My highlight was an over-the-head-catch of a pop fly in short right field that was the final out of one of our few wins.

Another member of our church, Mr. Harry Bittlinger, was the scout master of troop fifty-seven. The troop was sponsored by our church and met at A. B. Hill School, which I attended. Several of my friends were members of troop fifty-seven: Bobby Ginnaven, Roy Szekeley, and Barry Bright, so I joined up too. Scouting was a lot of fun and a great learning experience. We learned first aid, which included how to stop bleeding, different kinds of bandages, tourniquets, etc. The most fun times were the trips to Camp Currier in Mississippi. We would camp out for several days, learning to take care of ourselves, but with the whole troop acting as one. Everybody helped everyone else. We always had a Sunday morning worship service and said thanks before each meal.

> "Those who listen to instruction will prosper. Those who trust the Lord will be happy."
>
> Proverbs 16:20

Spring 1949

I finally made Second Class Scout, and I had many good experiences. Thank you to Harry Bittlinger and the other Scout leaders.

1950–1951

Susan turned four years old: cute, full of energy, and always wanting to be with me. Mom and Dad were still busy making a family. I was doing well in school, making the honor roll. I joined the Russell Reeves Oldsmobile Co. team in the Exchange Club baseball league. This team was coached by Ervin Crockett. I would play for Mr. Crockett for the next three years. We were building a team to make a run at the Memphis City Championship. The 1950 Russell Reeves team had some of my friends on it who would be friends for a lifetime: Bobby Emmons, Billy Atkins, Bob Ginnaven. We did okay and made it to the city playoffs, but got eliminated early.

> "Even strong young lions sometimes go hungry, but those who trust the Lord will never lack any good thing."
>
> Proverbs 34:10

Summer 1951

Our team was now sponsored by Goodyear (the tire maker). Our manager, Mr. Crockett, really worked hard to get them to be so generous to a bunch of little boys in South Memphis. Thank you, Goodyear!

We had a good season. Players like Bill and Tom Lowrey, Billy Atkins, Jimmy Loosier, along with myself, made it to the city playoffs but came up short again. We have been building a strong base for our team, and we have high expectations for 1952.

> "Happy are people of integrity, who follow the law of the Lord."
>
> Psalms 119:1

Goodyear Baseball Team
1952 Junior League City Champs

Fall 1951

Coach Ben Philbeck at A. B. Hill School got me to come out for football. This was my first time to play organized football. We played in the South Memphis Pee-Wee League. It consisted of A. B. Hill, Lauderdale, Cummings, Riverside, Mallory Heights, Longview Heights and Pine Hill.

1952

I was finishing the seventh grade at A. B. Hill School, active in scouting, church, and sports. I could hardly wait for baseball season, in anticipation of a great year. We started practice April 1. Mr. Crockett had Goodyear lined up as our sponsor for another season. Goodyear provided our uniforms in their blue, yellow, and white colors with

Goodyear across the front of our shirts. They also provided us with wooden bats, balls, catcher's equipment, and all of our Memphis park commission fees.

1952 *Baseball*

Mr. Crockett got our Goodyear team together in April. We would play at South Side Park in the Exchange Club sponsored by Junior League. Our team was sponsored by Goodyear Tire and Rubber Company. Other teams were the Yellow Cab, Kelsey Chevrolet, and J.T. Lamb. Our new league schedule included teams from West Memphis, Arkansas; Bartlett, Tennessee; Batesville, Mississippi; and any local teams that would play us. Our roster consisted of Billy Atkins, Jimmy Loosier, Jerry Dlugach, Earl Porter, Artie Clark, Buddy Clark, Robert Shelton, Tommy Crawford, Eugene Mosier, Bobby Atkins, Butch Dlugach, Jack House, Louis Dalton, and me. Our batboy, John Strange, was a young boy who was not old enough to play.

The summer of '52 was a dream come true for this group of boys from the working class neighborhood of South Memphis. By the time our preseason schedule was over, we were 16–0 and had beaten teams from Levi, Whitehaven, Oak Park, Oakville, and others. Our regular season started about the last week of May. We played each team four times, which made twelve league games. During this same period, we played six more exhibition games against teams from Millington, Bolton, Cordova, and others. By the time our regular season was over, we had won thirty-four and lost zero.

"Trust in the Lord always, for the Lord God is the eternal rock."

Isaiah 26:4

Billy Atkins, Jim Loosier, and Jerry Dlugach were all batting over 400. Artie Clark and Earl Porter were batting over 300, and Buddy Clark, Robert Shelton, Tommy Crawford were over 250. Louie Dalton, Butch Dlugach, Bobby "Blue Eyes" Atkins, and Eugene Mosier all filled in well. Jack House had to leave the team in July as his dad was transferred to Buffalo, New York. Oh, I almost forgot. I hit over 650 for the entire season. I had sixteen home runs, Atkins and Loosier had five home runs, and Dlugach and Porter had two home runs. The team spent almost every waking hour together. When we were not playing baseball, we went swimming at Maywood or Bare Creek, spent the night together mostly at my house, and helped each other mow the grass.

It was now time for the city championship playoffs. We opened up against St. Thomas from the Knights of Columbus League. They had a good team with players like Frank Krause, Bobby Ragsdale, and others. Mr. Crockett decided to start Dlugach as Goodyear's pitcher. St. Thomas got a lead and Goodyear could not catch up as Krause pitched a good game. This was Goodyear's first loss of the year. This was a real awakening, but because the city playoffs were double elimination, we had one more chance.

TELEVISION STAR—Joe Cooper made his video debut in auspicious fashion yesterday at Bellevue Park as he clouted two home runs to account for all his team's scoring as Goodyear defeated McLean Baptist 4-1 in a junior tournament of champions game. The game was carried by WMCT, The Commercial Appeal television station.
—Staff Photo

Goodyear's next three games were against teams from the Rotary, Optimist, and Lion's Leagues. I pitched two of the games and Dlugach and Porter the other. Goodyear won them all, making our record 37–1. After a weekend of rest, it was time for Goodyear to play St. Thomas again. This game I pitched and shut out St. Thomas on one hit. St. Thomas was eliminated. There were only two teams left: Goodyear with one loss and McLean Baptist with no losses. McLean had super players: Charlie Pierce, Darrell Guyman, the Perry boys, and others. Goodyear would have to beat McLean two times for the championship.

The first game was scheduled on Saturday afternoon. This was such a big event that the game was played at Bellevue Park, where state high schools and amateur games along with semi-pro championships were played. Bellevue had covered bleachers and seating for about 2,000 fans. Channel Five television carried the game live. The sports crew for Channel Five did the announcing, along with Mr. Hale from the Memphis Park Commission. Dlugach started as the Goodyear pitcher against Pierce from McLean. I was at third base.

In the second inning, McLean started to get to Dlugach and Goodyear fell behind. Mr. Crockett came out of the dugout and brought me in to pitch. McLean got no more hits or runs. With the rest of the Goodyear team getting on base, I hit two long home runs, winning the game for Goodyear. The television announcers went crazy. They had never expected so much excitement and entertainment from these young boys. Mr. Hale, one of the TV announcers, got the Goodyear team around me as

I was interviewed on live TV. So, today when you watch the Little League World Series, remember it all started at Bellevue Park in Memphis, Tennessee in 1952. The win meant that Goodyear and McLean would play again on Monday. Each had one loss. The city championship was played at the Fairgrounds Baseball Complex in early August.

McLean Baptist vs. Goodyear. The Goodyear team took up like they did in Saturday's game. Artie Clark, J. Dlugach, Earl Porter, Billy Atkins, Jimmy Loosier, Buddy Clark, Robert Shelton, and Tommy Crawford all got hits and walks, and I hit a double and two home runs again. I pitched and struck out twelve batters. All the younger boys, Bobby Atkins ("Blue Eyes"), Butch Dlugach, Mo Mosier, and Louie Dalton, got to play in the championship game. Goodyear Record: 40–1. The pitcher stats for the season were: Earl Porter 2–0, Jerry Dlugach 12–1, Joe Cooper 26–0. I had over 250 strikeouts, pitched fourteen no hitters, and had two perfect games.

The Exchange Club of Memphis gave our team a banquet at a fancy place downtown. They presented each of us with jackets that said "City Champs 1952" in the blue and gold Goodyear colors. It was a storybook summer, thanks to our mamas Molly Clark, Derlean Atkins, Betty Loosier, Mrs. Dlugach, Mrs. Dalton, and Mama Cooper and our number-one cheerleader, Susan Cooper.

"Give thanks to the Lord, for he is good! His faithful love lasts forever."

Psalm 103:1

Late Summer, 1952

As in all neighborhoods, there are those who want to bully the other kids. Poochie McCampbell and Paul Sumerall were our bullies.

This was also about the time when I admitted to myself that Harold Cooper, my dad, was a bully. Harold had never accepted me and whipped me with a leather strap for any slight misdeed and many times, for nothing at all. Apparently this was to just keep me fearful of him, and I was so scared that I had a continuous stomach ache whenever Harold was around.

For example, I was a bed wetter. Every night Harold would whip me for wetting the bed. I was made to sleep on an army cot. An army cot is made up of eight wood pieces with canvas stretched between them. Sometimes Harold would wake me up and make me stand in a corner the rest of the night. This went on until I was eleven or twelve years old, when I quit bed-wetting. I had house chores, such as keeping my clothes and things in order, carrying out the trash, keeping trash cans clean, mowing the grass, and helping with the maintenance of the house. If there was any slight miscue in any of these, I got whipped.

Harold Cooper never gave me a hug or kiss. Never!

I was active in scouting, church, sports and made good grades at school. This still did not get Harold off my back.

The only Little League baseball game Harold ever came to was the city championship game. I had hoped this would finally make Harold proud and ease the tension at home. Nothing changed. Harold was just as mean as ever.

Number 1 Cheerleader

Harold was also not very nice to my mother, always badgering her about something and making her cry. One time he pushed her down, and I jumped on his back. He slammed me into a wall, but he did leave Mom alone.

No matter how hard I tried to please Harold, nothing worked. In my teenage years, Harold traveled a lot. Weekdays were pleasant for Mom, Susan, and me, but the weekends were *hell*.

This meanness from Harold continued when I got my driver's license. Mostly I was to run errands for Harold, but if I had a date and needed the car, then Harold's "power trip" took over. "Why should I let you use my car?"

In 1956, I received an athletic scholarship to Memphis State (now University of Memphis). Harold, Mom and Susan drove me to Memphis State. We all got out where Coach Bob Henderson was greeting freshmen. Harold opened the car trunk and threw my old green duffle bag, with all my belongings, onto the sidewalk and said, "Coach, he's yours." I had never seen Harold Cooper so happy. *He was rid of me.*

Why did I put this reference to Harold Cooper at this time? From the eighth grade forward you will see a gradual change in the life of Joe Cooper. I think knowing about Harold, and how I was treated as a child and teenager, will help explain the change.

"Yet what we suffer now is nothing compared to the glory he will give us later."

Romans 8:18

Patty Sue

Continuing with the eighth grade, A. B. Hill School was alive with activities: paper drives, spaghetti suppers, talent shows, spelling bees, and even football, basketball, baseball for boys, and cheerleading and basketball for girls. My mom coached the girls' basketball. She had players like Ann Stoddard, Sylvia Hurdle, and Jeanine Goad. They had a really good team.

A new social event about this time was house parties chaperoned by parents. We would meet at someone's house and have chips and cokes. We played a game called Spin the Bottle. Everyone got in a circle, and a girl was in the middle. She would lay an empty bottle on the floor and spin it around. Whatever boy it pointed to, she had to kiss. Barbara Bruce, Carolyn Morrison, Sylvia Hurdle, Barbara Wiseman, and Beverly Salmon were some of the girls. Willie Cross, Marion Landers, Sonny Kendrick, Freddie Barrett, and I were the boys. It was harmless because we were all shy, and this introduction to boy-girl activities was new to us. Also, no one knew a thing about kissing.

A young lady, Patty Sue McCaskil, lived on Trigg Avenue. I thought she was really pretty and nice. I would sometimes walk over to Patty's house in the evening. Patty and I would sit on the front porch and talk. We were closely monitored by Mrs. McCaskil and Patty's older brother, Robert. *No touching, no kissing.* Patty Sue passed away early in her adult life. She is greatly missed. Robert is still my friend today.

During these early years, my friends and I spent summer days at South Side Park. There were always a couple of older high school or college students, called park directors, who watched the younger kids and had many activities scheduled for them to do: swings, slides, box hockey, left field ball, and a small pool.

The boys, who were older and athletes at South Side High School, would hang around the park sometimes. The ball players were always initiating us younger boys. They would get us to the top of the slide and then not let us slide down. They would catch us in the pool and hold our heads under the water until we lost all our breath and the bubbles quit coming up. Several would circle around us and make us try to get out of the circle. All of this was really in fun and made us tougher when we got to SSHS. Bill Key, Buster Turner, Rusty Brown, Sidney Bonner were some of those who did this. All became lifelong friends.

"Never be lazy in your work, but serve the Lord enthusiastically."

Romans 12:11

The 1952 athletic calendar at A. B. Hill was filled with excitement. Our football team, with Willie Cross, Sonny Kendrick, Hamp Hardy, Marion Landers, and Bobby Emmons, lost one game. My basketball team, with Emmons, Cross, Hardy, and Freddie Barnett, went undefeated. Softball and baseball were also successful.

The girls' basketball team, coached by Mama Cooper,

also won the championship. They were led by Anne Stoddard, Jeaninne Goad, and Sylvia Hurdle.

Spring of 1953

Looking back, this is about the time things in my personal life really started to change: puberty, mental, and physical changes. We finished up the school year and were promoted to the ninth grade at South Side High School. About this time, Harold told me to get a morning paper route. I had to get up at three a.m., walk three blocks to pick up the papers, and three more blocks to throw them door to door. On Friday evening, I went door to door to collect from the customer. I had 120 papers to throw and only about thirty of the customers paid on time. It was discouraging to me, who had gotten up all week and delivered *The Commercial Appeal,* to be avoided by the customers on Friday.

The money was due to *The Commercial Appeal* on Saturday morning. Most weeks, I had to take out of my own savings to pay and then spend all day Saturday trying to collect. You could hear people talking inside the house, but when you knocked and said, "Paperboy," everything got quiet, and no one would come to the door.

I would be two or three houses away and see a customer go into his house. When I would knock and identify myself, no one would come to the door. Others would say, "Come back later." Some would be drunk and talk nasty to me. This all made for an unpleasant experience. Shortly thereafter, I had an attack of appendicitis and

JOSEPH M. COOPER, SR.

surgery. The manager of the delivery department gave my route to another person. *Amen!*

The 9th Grade, South Side High School–"The Scrappers"

I already had lots of friends at SSHS, so the transition from A. B. Hill went easily. Senior girls, who knew me from sports or South Side Park, now worked as student helpers in the school office. They helped me get acquainted with the principal, Mr. Wadley, and his staff, Mrs. Boyd and Mrs. McGoldrick, and with my schedule and teachers. These two girls, Anne Threlkeld and Regina Facinelli, now Anne Brawer and Regina Boyd, are still friends today.

School was good. I played quarterback on the freshman football team, and that was the beginning of my participation in football, basketball, track, and baseball for SSHS for four years. I got four letters each year for a total of twelve. Our freshman football won six, lost one.

My SSHS freshmen 1953 basketball team, with Bobby Emmons, Willie Cross, Don Lutz, Walter Reitano, Billy Atkins, and Billy Terrell won the freshmen city championship. I was voted Most Valuable Player of the tournament.

Probably in early 1954, I began to realize that other dads cared about their children and were supportive of them, and Harold Cooper seemed only to make life miserable for me. A few of these dads were Mr. Buddy Atkins (Billy and Blue Eyes), Mr. Jim Echols (James and Robert), Mr. Emmons (Bobby and Willie), Nelson

Roberts (Joe and Phyllis), and Harry Billinger (Harry, Joe). They were examples of loving fathers.

> "Love does no wrong to anyone, so love satisfies all of God's requirements."
>
> Romans 13:10

Fourteen years old, finishing the ninth grade, and I was growing up. I started noticing girls more seriously, and they me.

Spring football at SSHS brought a change in coaches. Hickman "Hick" Ewing, a Memphis South Side High School coaching legend, was appointed Shelby County Clerk. The new coach was Jack Stribling. He had played at Old Miss and was an all-sec end. Coach Stribling also brought a new offense, the T-formation. Coach Ewing was a single-wing/Notre Dame box offensive genius. As a sophomore-to-be, I and my ninth grade teammates got to be the practice dummies in spring football. This was a toughening experience.

I was becoming more aggressive and getting tired of being bullied. I found out that my even manner was mistaken for weakness—in South Memphis words, a "Chicken xxxx."

One of the neighborhood bullies pushed me in front of some other boys, and I tripped over the curb and fell to the ground. No one expected what came next as I got up and proceeded to pound on the bully, knocking him into a storm sewer. Shortly thereafter, another boy named Frank slapped me in the face. I wrestled Frank to the ground and hit him until he was pulled off. Frank stayed away from me after that.

Freshman Baseball 1954

I pitched a one-hitter against CHS for the city championship, and also had two hits. My record was three wins and zero losses. This was also when I learned about the sport of track. Coaches Ollie Smith and Stribling did a good job, as the young boys picked up the sport easily.

Billy Terrell and I had girlfriends who lived close to one another on Laclede Street. We walked together on weekends to see them. My friend was Betty Ann and Billy's was Harriet.

Summer of 1954

I moved up to varsity baseball from the American Legion sponsored league. Teams from the local high schools competed against one another. Our sponsor was Pepsi Cola.

I was now taking care of the mowing and trimming at Parkway Methodist Church, which would be my job for the next couple of years. Harold Cooper also had me walking through the surrounding neighborhoods pushing my lawnmower and knocking on doors to cut yards.

Legion baseball was a good experience. Our coach, Russell Brigance, had been my freshman football and basketball coach, but he was now the varsity baseball coach. I pitched some with two wins, one loss record and was a utility player whenever Coach needed me.

"He restoreth my soul: he leadeth me in the paths of righteousness for his name's sake. Yea, though I walk through the valley of the shadow of death, I will fear no evil: for thou art with me; thy rod and thy staff they comfort me."

Psalm 24:3-4

Coach knew of some of my problems with Harold Cooper, and he was always supportive and helpful. Mattie always came to our games and cheered for us. She became dear friends with my mom. A love and respect between Coach Brigance, Mama Mattie (as we later called her), and me still exists. Coach passed away several years ago, but Mama Mattie is still with us.

"God puts those in our lives who ease the pain that some-one else has caused us."

Joe Cooper

August 1954, Bobby Emmons got a car, and so did Hamp Hardy. Although they were in the same school grade as me, they were a year older. With their cars we had the opportunity to be more mobile. Marion Landers, Bobby, Hamp, and I would get some of the local girls to go to the movies (mostly Bellevue Drive-In), Leonard's Bar-B-Q, or Gus' Place. Betty Ann, Ginger, Carol, Cathy, Dot, and Linda were some of the girls we hung out with.

Football practice started. It was 100° and the coaches were working us hard. Our team went to Shelby Forest State Park for a week of intense practice and offense–defense study. I pulled a hamstring muscle, but kept practicing. We had a good team with players like Erle Merriman, Fred Hearn, Bill Evans, and others. We lost the championship on Thanksgiving Day to Central High School in the famous "stopped clock game." With only a few seconds left, the game was tied. Central had the ball, and for some still unknown reason, the clock kept stopping. Central got two extra plays because of this. On the last play, our defensive back fell down, and Central scored for the win.

I got to play some as a sophomore and establish myself as a leader and player. Other things were going okay. School was especially interesting. The algebra teacher, Miss Gordon, was flabbergasted at my ability to do all the work so easily. She would send me to the blackboard to do the day's assignment for the class. Finally she asked how I did it, and I told her my mom was a math and science master. The students in the class had known this all the time.

Miss Allensworth, an elderly English teacher, was always having pranks pulled on her. Her classroom was on the third floor of SSHS. While she was out of the room, John Sanders slipped out and lay down below the classroom windows. All the students gathered by the windows. When Miss Allensworth came back and asked, "What's going on?" the class told her that John had jumped out of the window. She ran screaming to the window and looked down below to see John lying on the ground. She almost fainted. The class all was rolling in the aisles with laughter. Many of us got in trouble that day.

Basketball Season

I played a lot as a sophomore on the varsity squad, and by tournament time, I had demonstrated my ability to play with the older boys. One highlight was when Frayser High School came to SSHS to play. Frayser was loaded with talent, especially a set of twins who could really play. One of these boys was scoring a basket every time he touched the ball. Coach Smith had tried several players to guard this boy, and finally he said, "Cooper, get on him and shut him down." I was all over this Frayser player and held him with only two points for the remainder of the game.

1955 *Spring Football Practice*

The coaches, Stribling, Smith, Brigance, Jimmy Crawford, and Bill Stribling (Coach Jack's brother who played pro ball for the New York Giants), were trying to figure out which players to put on the field for SSHS. Floyd Massey, Jerry "Meatball" Davis, John Sanders, Bobby Webb, Maury Phillips, Dick Sutton, James "Snake" Echols, Red Palmer, Billy Landers, Charlie Huckaby, were the main seniors-to-be. Sam Locastro, Jim Loosier, Tommy Clinton, Ed Watson, Sonny Kendrick, Billy Atkins, David Pittman, and I were the juniors who would be playing.

As the practice progressed, I became a starter at defensive half-back, along with being the back-up to Huckaby at QB, and Landers at HB on offense.

Baseball, Spring 1955

We were a solid team, but since our senior pitching was weak, we finished behind Treadwell and Central.

Track season is short, but Red Palmer, Billy Landers, Bobby Webb, Erle Merriman, Jim Loosier, Tommy Clinton, and I all qualified for the district and regional meets.

> "From my experience, I know that fools who turn from God may be successful for the moment, but then comes sudden disaster."
>
> Job 5:3

Other than school and sports, my life was changing. I was no longer active in scouting. I only went to church because I was made to, and even then I did not pay attention. About the time that school was out in 1955, Marion Landers, Hamp Hardy, and I were out one night in Hamp's car. The Cotton Carnival, a huge event with many parties and a Midway Fair, was going on. By the way, now the boys knew who would sell beer to the football players at SSHS. Hamp, Marion, and I got a couple of quarts of Falstaff and headed to the Midway. There were a lot of girls out at the Cotton Carnival, and it was not long before we hooked up with some of them. We drove to Riverside Park, which overlooks the Mississippi River, and started making out. Afterwards, as we were leaving the park, I drove off and ran into a ditch. We were not hurt, but we could not get the car out of the ditch. The girls caught a city bus home. Hamp, Marion, and

I were scared to go home, so we slept in a cotton shed and went home the next day. Marion and Hamp's parents were glad to see them and talked to them about not doing such things. I was welcomed home by my mom and Susan, but Harold Cooper took me to the police station and juvenile court as if I were a criminal. This incident made me understand even more how I was treated differently than my peers.

There was an older girl who lived not too far from me. Both her parents were gone in the daytime, and this girl would get me to come over. She introduced me to real sex. I was fifteen at that time.

Sixteen Years Old, Summer 1955

I had a job painting a house and working at the Memphis Zoo on weekends.

American Legion baseball was in session and our South Side team was again competitive. I pitched and played utility again, along with any place Coach Brigance needed me. CBC, Central, Treadwell, and South Side all competed to be number one. I had five wins, one loss for the season, and hit 303.

Evenings were spent at Leonard's B-B-Q at Bellevue and McLemore or Gus' Place on Bellevue and Kerr, hanging out, drinking beer, picking up girls, and making out. Usually, the beer was free because we played football for South Side.

I had been saving money since my first job cutting yards, delivering papers, and selling Cokes at the college football games at Crump Stadium. Once, Tennessee, Ole Miss, Vanderbilt, and Kentucky played a day-night doubleheader. I made $27 working both games, which was my best day. After getting money from painting the house, I wanted to get a cheap car. My mom said she was okay with the idea, as it would make it easier for me to get to school, ball practice, dates, and games. Harold caused an argument and said it would be over his dead body before I got a car. By now, I had my driver's license, but only occasionally was I allowed to use the family car.

Preseason Football, 1955

After a week of practice at SSHS, we were off to Shelby Forest for a week of camp. Coach Stribling and his staff put us through a tough week. Bobby Webb was overcome with heat and several others threw up, but all in all, we had a great week. We scrimmaged Ripley, Tennessee High School on Saturday, then headed home.

School started on the day after Labor Day. The next Friday, we opened our season in Chattanooga, Tennessee, playing another powerhouse, Chattanooga Central High School: The Purple Pounders. It was a great game. The Purple Pounders beat the Scrappers by a touchdown. I was starting as defensive back and as backup at QB and HB on offense.

Against Messick High School, I took a pitch out and faked a run to the right, stopped and hit a streaking Floyd Massey with a fifty-yard touchdown pass for the win. In other games, I would pass to James Echols for the winning score, pitch to Red Palmer, Billy Landers, and hand off to the bulldozer Bobby Webb to score. It was a great season for the Scrappers, except we had a player who came in before the season and provided eligibility papers that were fraudulent. This kept SSHS out of the championship game. Our wonderful cheerleaders were led by Virginia Hill, Gloria Reading, and Sue Caldwell.

By now it's Thanksgiving, 1955. I am 6 ft., 175 lbs. and very good looking. The girls are really after me, the handsome star athlete. I had it made, but I also liked to have a few beers with the older men and became basically inactive in church.

> "Then I realized that God allows people to continue in their sinful ways so he can test them."
>
> Ecclesiastes 3:18

Team Managers and Trainers

Dr. Sidney Vick, a local M.D., would work with the trainers to give them basic first aid and such. Dr. Vick also gave the Scrappers their required physicals. He did this all as a free service. Byron Evans, John Shanks, Nelson Tucker, Henry "Herky" Alexander, John Echols, and others were the managers/trainers. These guys kept all the equipment and uniforms clean and ready. They also kept minor injuries treated, ankles taped, and water and salt tablets available. The water was available only after practice, as this was before athletes were allowed water while practicing. Also no water bottles during games.

Byron Evans learned well as he went to on Memphis State University as a manager/trainer. Nelson Tucker was always pulling pranks and jokes on the players. Once he put analgesic in with Vaseline and gave it to Carroll Langston to use for jock itch. About five minutes later, Langston was on fire. After getting the rub off, Langston and some more players tied Tucker up and put him in the shower with the cold water running. When Coach Ollie Smith came to shower, he found Tucker nearly frozen. Another time Nelson Tucker put a rubber snake in James Echols locker while we were on the practice field. When James opened his locker, the snake fell out scaring James and everyone around. Echols, Bobby Webb, and others tied Nelson up, put him in the dirty laundry cart, piled dirty shorts, jerseys, and socks on him. Again, Coach Smith found him and set him free. Nelson Tucker went on to become an electrician. He worked on the Alaskan pipelines and did the wiring of the Memphis Arkansas Bridge. Today he is retired and trains horses. Henry Alexander and John Echols went on to graduate from college and live successful lives.

The Scrapper Booster Club is made up of former Scrappers, community leaders, parents, and supporters. The Booster Club had been active for years. They supplied Scrapper athletes with many of the things needed to have a successful program: uniforms, balls, shoes, transportation to games, football camp, and on and on. Skeeter Motes, Don Arwood, Bedford Calhoun, Rudy Malone, Bubba Blackwell, Earl Dykema, Dr. Vick, and every business in South Memphis supported the Scrappers. There are booster clubs all over the USA that have some influence or heritage from the South Side Scrapper Booster Club.

Winter of 1955

Basketball Season–Bobby Emmons (who could hit a two-hand set shot from twenty-five feet all day long) and Hamp Hardy left school and joined the military. I was a starting forward along with Billy Landers, Jerry Davis, Pete Lyon, and Charly Huckaby. Others were J. W. Adams, Robert Echols, Earl Porter, Billy Terrell, Buddy Wise, and Willie Cross. Coach Ollie Smith kept us on our toes. The Scrappers had a winning season, and we made it through the playoffs until CBC, led by Big Bill Lowrey, 6 ft., 7 in. center, eliminated us. I had an exciting season, averaging ten points and five rebounds per game.

Mr. Clark, Sr., Artie Clark's grandfather, was a contractor. He built new houses and did renovations. He always had some work for me like tacking bricks, sanding boards, rubbing paneling, and cleaning up the job site for some extra money. I worked some for Mr. Clark in 1955–1956. During the winter of '55, weekend nights were "date nights." Several couples would be at the Bethune Drive-In Movie. Car windows would be fogged up, and no one ever saw a movie.

Spring Football, 1956

The Scrappers had many returning players: Sonny Kendrick, Danny Spercia, Allen Herring, Sam LoCastro, Buddy Shanks, Ed Watson, Marion Landers, Glen Moore, Willie Cross, Tommy Clinton, Jimmy Loosier, Terry Jeans, David Pittman, Walter Reitano, Skipper Creamer, Richard Presley, and me. The juniors-to-be were Carroll Langston, Robert Echols, J. W. Adams, and

Don Lewis. We had a good spring practice and were excited about our coming season.

An older man who was always at our games had a beer joint over by the Mississippi River near the Harrahan Bridge. Some of my friends and I would go there to drink beer and be entertained by the older women. When the police came by, we would go into the kitchen. I was just seventeen years old and learning some bad habits. By now the only time I went to church was when there was nothing else to do.

Baseball and Track, 1956

The Scrappers were good. Coach Brigance had John Sanders, Billy Landers, Jerry Davis, Herbie Ashworth, and others to go along with me. SSHA played for the championship right up until the final week of the season. In pitching I had five wins, one loss, and batted over 300 as a utility player.

Track was a success as Billy Landers, Red Palmer, Bobby Webb, Tommy Clinton, and I each won medals in the medley relay, 880 relay, and mile relay in the state meet.

School Year Ending, 1956

Many of my best friends graduated from SSHS: Floyd Massey, James Echols, Charlie Huckaby, John Sanders, Ed Baker, Al Sanders, and Red Palmer. We had not only been teammates, but we had a lot of other fun times. We would go to a place where they were selling watermelons. One of us would distract the attendant, and two of us would snatch watermelons and run back to the car.

While the attendant was trying to catch the two who had the melons, the distracter would run the other way, and we would pick him up. We would take the watermelons back to South Side Park and have a feast. Pete Sanders, John's older brother, would meet us sometimes and tell jokes for hours that kept us all laughing. Other times we would climb the fence at Pine Hill swimming pool at night and swim naked. We had a lot of good times.

"Don't let the excitement of youth cause you to forget your creator."

Ecclesiastes 12:1

1956 All-Legion Team

Summer, 1956

I was back working at the Memphis Zoo. My main job was making snow cones. I still had to hitch a ride across town from South Memphis or ride the city bus. Even though I had saved money, Harold Cooper still refused to let me have a car.

Friends like Ed Watson, Billy Atkins, Billy Terrell, Jim Loosier, Carroll Langston, and Roy Adams helped me get around. They all had old but dependable cars that they had bought with their savings.

American Legion Baseball

Pepsi Cola was again SSHS sponsor. Tommy Clinton, Jim Loosier, J. W. Adams, Billy Terrell, Don Lewis, Robert Echols, Tommy Cox, Earl Porter, Dan Melton, Willie Cross, Billy Atkins, and I are Coach Brigance's boys. We played teams from around the Memphis area along with our Legion schedule. Everyone played well, and Pepsi Cola challenged teams from CBC, Treadwell, Central, and Messick for the title. I had seven wins, three losses pitching, and over 300 hits.

Another place that my friends and I hung out was Dixie Ice Cream, a small hamburger and ice cream joint close to SSHS. Mr. and Mrs. Neri operated this business, and they were very good to all the SSHS students. One time Billy Terrell, J.W. Adams, Marion Landers, and I were at Neri's place when the drink supply truck came. I grabbed two six packs of Pepsi off the truck and took off. The police found us at Milton Hatcher's barbershop, and because Leo, the drink truck driver insisted, Billy Terrell and I were taken to juvenile. I told the police that J. W. was not involved, and they let him go. Everyone at juvenile was laughing at us for getting busted for doing such a silly thing. The officials sent us home to our parents.

My mom was mad at me for such a foolish thing, but she knew it was just in fun. Harold Cooper treated me as if I was a criminal, cursing and threatening me. As I was warming up for the game that night, Coach Brigance had to ask Harold to go back to the stands.

Leonard's, Gus,' and snatching watermelons were some of our evening activities. Most every night, I would hook up with some girl before going home. I would also pitch for one of the local semi-pro teams on the weekend. They played in places like Hernando, Batesville, and Senatobia, Mississippi; Dyersburg, Humbolt, or Brownsville, Tennessee. I would play under an assumed name and get $25 per game. As summer baseball was ending, some of the Scrapper footballers and I were working out at the Water Works, going over offensive plays, passing, kicking, and working on conditioning.

Football, 1956

The Scrappers started workouts with high expectations for the season. Coach Stribling, Smith, Mathis, Brigance, and team went off to Shelby Forest for a week of work: 6 a.m. run a mile, 7:30 a.m. breakfast, 9:30 a.m. practice for 2 ½ hours, into the pool, cool off. Then, put on shorts and t-shirts and go to lunch. Catch a nap. Then at 3:30 p.m., we were back onto the practice field until 6 p.m., shower, then supper. Team meetings were after supper when we would go over offense and defense assignments. This team really came together at camp. I was chosen captain of the team and David Pittman, co-captain, by the team members. On Saturday, the last day of camp, the Scrappers outscored the

Ripley team in a scrimmage. Back to South Memphis for Saturday night, some beer, girls, and hanging out.

All of South Memphis was excited about the upcoming season. The team members and I were the pride of all Scrapper fans. We traveled to Chattanooga again for a rematch with the Purple Pounders of Chattanooga Central. It was the season opener for both teams. Cooper and Langston scored touchdowns, and Skipper Creamer kicked a game-winning field goal. That was a huge win as the Pounders had not lost in two years and were the 1955 Sports Writers' Number One in Tennessee.

We were back home at Crump Stadium the next Friday night. It was SSHS vs. Catholic High School. The Scrapper offensive line did a great job. Cooper, Langston, and Loosier ran the ball well, and Atkins, Adams, Clinton, and Cross all caught passes from me. SSHS 33–Catholic High School 13. Frank Canale, Jerry Findley, and Julian Hayes played well for Catholic.

South Side Scrappers Vs. CBC Purple Wave
September 20th, 1956

SOUTH SIDE HIGH SCHOOL STARTING LINEUP

No.	Name	Pos.
89	ATKINS	LE
73	KINDRICKS	LT
65	SHANKS	LG
55	WATSON	C
68	LOCASTRO	RG
87	REITANO	RT
81	ADAMS	RE
10	COOPER	QB
34	CLINTON	LH
20	LANGSTON	RH
45	LOOSIER	FB

CBC High School STARTING LINEUP

No.	Name	Pos.
30	Ritten	L.E.
76	Fracchia	L.T.
62	O'Neil	L.G.
51	Ekmark	C.
33	Brennan	R.G.
77	Mohr	R.T.
73	McCarver	R.E.
12	Menzer	Q.B.
31	Abraham	L.H.
23	Massey	R.H.
60	Soefker	F.B.

SOUTH SIDE HIGH FOOTBALL ROSTER

No.	Name	Position	No.	Name	Position	No.	Name	Position
10	COOPER (Capt.)	QB	45	LOOSIER	B	74	YOUNG	E
12	ECHOLS	QB	51	PRINCE	C	75	BRYANT	T
16	ROBERTS	QB	52	KIRKSEY	C	76	HERRING	T
20	LANGSTON	B	53	HOPPER	C	77	SPENCER	T
21	VAILLANCOURT	B	55	WATSON	C	78	LOCASTRO, T.	T
24	MERRYMAN	B	60	MONTGOMERY	G	81	ADAMS	E
25	JEANES	B	62	NANCE	G	82	FOX	E
31	MADDOX	B	63	PRESSLEY, T.	G	83	TRUSS	E
32	TAYLOR, S.	B	64	POFF	G	84	CREAMER	E
33	TEMPFER	B	65	SHANKS	G	85	PRESSLEY, R.	E
34	CLINTON	B	66	CLEMENTS	G	86	WISE	E
35	LEWIS	B	68	LOCASTRO, S.	G	87	REITANO	E
40	SELBY	B	69	MOORE	G	88	CROSS	E
41	TAYLOR, J.	B	71	BARCHERT	T	89	ATKINS	E
42	PITTMAN (Ah. C.)	B	72	HATCHER	T			
44	CHANDLER	B	73	KINDRICKS	T			

CBC HIGH SCHOOL ROSTER

No.	Name	Pos.	No.	Name	Pos.	No.	Name	Pos.
12	Menzer, E., Co-Capt.	QB	43	Grooms, J.	C	68	Grisanti	T
14	Robinson, T. J.	QB	47	Robilio, J. Fred	C	70	Kuhn, P.	T
15	Truemper, L.	QB	49	Kyle, R.	G	71	Guldi, J.	T
20	Gilia	B	50	Canale, T.	G	72	Mitchell, W.	T
21	Brannan, F.	C	51	Ekmark, K., Captain	C	73	McCarver, T.	E
22	Ross, I.	B	52	Morgan, K.	B	74	Patton, E.	B
27	George, W.	QB	54	Baugh, W.	B	75	Bittman, L.	C
30	Ritten, P.	E	60	Soefker, W.	B	76	Fracchia, F.	T
31	Abraham, S.	B	61	O'Neil, R.	E	77	Mohr, G.	T
32	Robinson, T. C.	B	62	O'Neil, B.	G	81	Kinney, J.	B
33	Brennan, C.	B	63	Fury, I.	B	82	Jolly, R.	T
34	McKenzie, E.	C	64	McAden, K.	E	83	Wright, T.	E
36	Isaacs, P.	E	65	Robinson, P.	G	85	Paccasassi, E.	E
40	Gillum, A.	G	66	Ragland, J.	B	84	Hawkins, R.	G
42	Johnson, J.	B	67	Brignole, M.	G	86	Taramangos, G.	G
						87	Askew, D.	B

Starting Line Up From Program

This was one of the all-time classic high school games ever played at E. H. Crump Stadium. There was standing room only in this arena where the University of Tennessee, Ole Miss, Vanderbilt, and other SEC teams play. CBC, led by Carl Ekmark, Buddy Soefker, Jim Johnson, Ronnie O'Neil, and others, scored first and led 6–0 as they missed the extra point. Finally, I scored for the Scrappers making it SSHS 6–CBC 6. Skipper Creamer again made the important extra point, and the Scrappers held on for a 7–6 victory. The Scrappers rolled on.

THE CHATTANOOGA TIMES: CHATTANOOGA, TENN., SATURDAY, SEPTEMBER 8, 1956.

Southside Trips Central 13-10---

MEMPHIANS RALLY TO SHADE 'ETTER'

Quarterback Scores All 10 Points in Loss Before 4,500 at Stadium

STATISTICS

By BOB WEATHERLY

Memphis' Southside Scrapper proved they were just that last night as they showed alternating bursts of speed and power in defeating the Purple Pounders of Central High 13-10 before an estimated crowd of 4,500 at Chamberlain Field.

Although Coach Red Etter's Dodds Avenue aggregation quickly jumped to a 7-0 lead, the Shelby Countians seemed to gain momentum as the game progressed and pushed over a tally each in the second and third quarters that provided their victory.

Quarterback Gene Etter, the Pounders' little magician, accounted for all of his team's points, scoring a touchdown in the first frame from one yard out, adding the extra point by placement and then kicking a 15-yard field goal in the second.

Carroll Langston, a fleet-footed halfback, scored one of the Scrappers' markers while Joe Cooper, captain and quarterback, added the other.

The Pounders got off to a lightning-like start, taking the opening kickoff and marching to score. Captain Benny Parks hauled in the ball on his 9 and raced back to the 31. From there Central churned goalward, completing the journey in 12 plays with Etter plunging over from the one for the touchdown. His placement was straight and high. Central led 7-0 and Pounder fandom sent noise washing down the stadium walls.

And it was not until late in the second quarter that Southside caught fire when Langston broke loose for an 11-yard jaunt from his 47 to Central's 42. Then the Scrappers began clicking.

—Times Staff Photo by Bob ?

CENTRAL GANGS MEMPHIS CAPTAIN JOE COOPER AFTER GAIN

Langston, Jimmy Loosier and Tommy Clinton, the latter a specialist on the belly play, shouldered the load with some shifty and deceptive running. Langston went the last eight yards—ramming the right side of the Central line for the marker. Charles Cramer's placement was wide and the Pounders still enjoyed a one-point advantage. It 4:20 until halftime.

After an exchange of punts, Central appeared to be well on its way again when center James Henley intercepted a Memphis pass on the Scrappers' 33. When Etter faded back for a pass, Memphis was penalized 15 yards for a personal foul and that stationed the Pounders on Memphis' 18. Etter then tried a lateral pass to John Davis but missed and suffered a 19-yard loss. It was this play that Coach Etter called the turning point of the game. Central managed to move back to the Scrappers' 15, where they decided to settle for Etter's field goal, which he made good, instead of gambling for a touchdown. The three-pointer came with five seconds left until the intermission and the Pounders led 10-6.

The Scrappers' clincher came with 2:58 remaining in the third quarter after a 56-yard sustained drive. Langston highlighted the trip with a 23-yard gallop and Cooper piled over from the 2 to score. Creamer's placement was good this time and that ended the night's point-making.

Central's running game received a severe jolt early in the first quarter when Capt. Benny Parks suffered a knee injury and was used afterwards only on defense as a sideback and also as an outside linebacker. He requested Coach Etter use him in a defensive role after discovering he was unable to run effectively. Thus, John Davis and James Reece bore the brunt of the Pounder attack, both breaking away several times for long gains.

Cooper handled the ball well for Memphis and was a smooth performer at the signal-calling post.

Central's band and drill squad put on a clever halftime show, with these features: a salute to the 1956 Pounders; to Coach Etter; to Memphis and all of the Pounders' West Tennessee friends and to Central.

MEMPHIS
Ends—Creamer, Wise, Atkins, Cross.
Tackles—Kindricks, B r y a n t, Boenser, Pox.
Guards—Nance, Pressler, Shanks, Locastro, Moore.
Centers—Prince, Watson.
Backs—Cooper, Echols, Langston, Jeanes, Teerafer, Clinton, Pittman, Loosier.
CENTRAL
Ends—McFraser, McGee, Aitchbrook.
Tackles—Waldrop, Freeman.
Guards—Henley, Lance, Kincier.
Backs—Etter, Jennings, Brown, Mallett, Parks, Reece, Keene, Cheek, Catson, Putnam, Davis.
Memphis Southside .. .. .. 0 6 7 2—15
Central ... ... 7 3 0 6—19
Memphis scoring: Touchdowns, Langston (8 yards); Cooper (2-yard run). Conversion, Creamer.
Central scoring: Touchdown, Etter (1-yard run). Conversion, Etter. Field goal, Etter.

On October 20, 1956, Moose Heart High School Red Ramblers from Moose Heart, Illinois, the 1955 Sports Writers' High School National Champion, came to town. This game was played on a Saturday night because a sell-out crowd was expected. Coach Stribling and his staff got us ready. The Booster Club, Bubba Blackwell, Rudy Malone, Don Arwood, and others told us how important this game was to the SSHS programs. The Scrappers came out on fire. Sam Locastro made a big hit on the first play, and Moose Heart fumbled. The Scrappers did not waste any time scoring. David Pittman, Terry Jeans, Langston, Clinton, and Cooper ran the ball. Kendrick, Shanks, Watson, Reitano, and Locastra blocked the Red Rambler to the ground. Jeans, Adams, Atkins, and Lewis all caught passes from Cooper and Robert Echols. All the juniors and sophomores got to play some. Final score: SSHS 44–Moose Heart 13.

After these games, there was

always a party, maybe at someone's home or at Riverside Park. These parties were after a visit to Leonard's Bar-B-Q and Gus' Place. Sometimes Mr. Neri would stay open late for us. Our great cheerleaders were Betty Mimms, Judy Compton, Mary Lipsey, Betty Ann Vandaventer, Donna Jackson, Alice Nelson, Loyce Stafford, Sally Taylor, Patsy Jones, Wilma Durham, Margaret Lipsey, Billy Terrell, Joe Hall, and Larry Gately. This group did super pep rallies, decorated our side of the stadium for games, and led all Scrapper fans in cheers and songs.

"A real friend sticks closer than a brother (or sister)."
Proverbs 18:24

The Scrappers continued through the schedule, and on Friday, November 30, 1956, played Messick High School in the thirteenth annual E. H. Crump Memorial Football Game for the blind.

A sold-out Crump Stadium was the scene of a bruising high school football battle. For the Messick Panthers, Richard Davis, Booth Tarkington, Jim Hampson, and Alex Saliba played well. The Scrapper defense, led by Reitano, Shanks, Pittman, and Watson, held the Panthers scoreless in the first half. The offense, with Clinton, Langston, and me, carried the ball, and Atkins, Cross, and Adams caught my passes and scored a touchdown. Creamer kicked the extra point for a SSHS 7, Messick High School 0 at halftime.

The halftime show featured a young man on his way to fame and fortune. Elvis Presley thrilled the crowd with a great performance, singing, shaking, and thrilling the fans. During the second half, the Panthers were still unable to move the ball, but the Scrappers lost a fumble and gave the Panthers an opportunity. Saliba led the Panthers to a tying touchdown when a Scrapper defender fell down on a pass. SSHS 7, Messick High School 7. Coach Stribling moved me to halfback and put Echols at QB. It only took these two and the Scrapper offensive blockers a short time to score. Echols ran a keeper for a first down and handed off to me on a counter play for a twenty-six-yard touchdown run. Skipper Creamer kicked the extra point. Final score: South Side Scrappers 14–Messick Panthers 7. This victory sealed the Memphis Prep League Championship for the Scrappers who were voted number one in Tennessee by the sports writers.

Scrapper footballers were the pride of South Memphis. The Booster Club gave us a great banquet; the Lions' Club of Shelby County honored the Scrappers for their victory and participation in the blind game. Our victory in the E. H. Crump Memorial sealed a bid for our junior and sophomore players in next year's Thanksgiving Day game. Several of the Scrappers received honors and athletic scholarships to college. After receiving offers from Vanderbilt, Tulane, Army, Navy, and several smaller high academic schools, Harold Cooper insisted that I sign with Memphis State. Coach Ralph Hatley, the head man at Memphis State, came to the Cooper house and did all the paperwork for me to sign. Mama Cooper, sister Susan, and Harold were also there. After the papers were signed, Coach Hatley gave me a ride downtown to the Black and

White Store where I had a job during Christmas break. Wilma Durham and a couple of other South Siders also worked there.

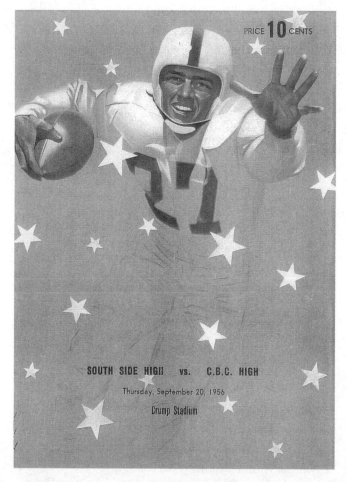

PRICE **10** CENTS

SOUTH SIDE HIGH vs. C.B.C. HIGH

Thursday, September 20, 1956

Crump Stadium

Copy of Program

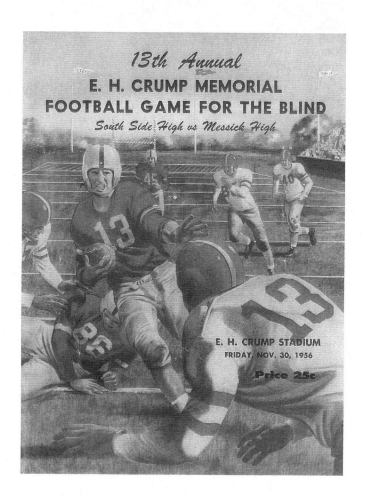

Joe Cooper Senior Picture 1956

Memphis Press-Scimitar

THURSDAY, JULY 16, 1964   SECOND SECTION—PAGE 25

Annoying Underpass on Lamar Is Finally Opened to Traffic

SMOOTH SAILING—But for 18 months it was rough riding. It's the new six-lane Southern Railway underpass on Lamar near McLean which was opened to traffic today. Patrolman J. M. Cooper (left), and R. N. Stratton were all smiles about it. They said some wrecks there had held up traffic for a half hour or more.
—*Press-Scimitar Staff Photo by William Leaptrot*

By MENNO DUERKSEN
Press-Scimitar Staff Writer

The Lamar-Southern railway underpass was finally opened to traffic today—after expense of $500,000, over 18 months of construction during which three lives were lost and there were 11 injuries and at least 30 wrecks there.

J. B. Michael Construction Co. took down the last barricades last night which allowed traffic to move down both sides of the street on six lanes.

The job is not officially completed, however, said Tennessee Highway Department. Another layer of asphalt is needed and the job must be inspected.

The underpass was originally scheduled for completion before the end of 1963. It was delayed last year when a barge load of fabricated steel sank in the Mississippi River.

Last December, three persons were killed and three injured in a violent crash when their car struck a center steel beam.

A number of motorists complained from time to time about inadequate lighting and warning signs.

"Boy, am I glad that job is finished," said City Traffic Engineer Robert Fosnaugh, whose office has been in charge of keeping traffic moving through the area.

Traffic was frequently bottle-necked at peak rush hours moving through one lane and on each side and sometimes just one lane.

Winter, 1957

Basketball season was underway. Billy Terrell, Robert Echols, Earl Porter, J. W. Adams, Walter Reitano, Willie Cross, and I were the varsity players. Buddy Wise, Terrell McNutt, and others also contributed. The Scrappers had a good season, but lost out to the Messick Panthers in the playoffs. I averaged fourteen points a game and six rebounds.

No spring football for me and the other seniors.

Track season and the Scrappers were again strong in the relays. Tommy Clinton, Terry Jeans, Jim Loosier, Don Lewis, Robert Echols, and I all won at least one medal in the state meet.

Baseball Memphis Prep League, 1957

Baseball has always been my favorite sport; I had dreams of playing pro ball. Scouts from the major league teams, Shakey Cain, Philadelphia; Buddy Lewis, Cardinals; Mr. Russo, Pittsburgh; and Hall of Fame Catcher Bill Dickey, Yankees all come to see me play. Coach Brigance had his squad from legion ball, Clinton, Loosier, Terrell, Atkins, Lewis, Echols, Cox, Adams, Melton, Porter, and me, ready to compete for the championship. The Scrappers worked their way to the state semi-finals against CBC. The winner played Kingsport for the Tennessee state title. I had seven wins, one loss for the season.

The loss came when the defense allowed three runs. Bellevue Park was packed, and the fans were standing down both foul lines; me from SSHS and Guido Grilli from CBC. We had been having pitching duels since little league. CBC also had Gene Giannini, Louis Bosi, Ray Mohler, Nathan Pera, and Tim McCarver (St. Louis Cardinals). Going into the sixth inning, South Side was winning 1–0 on a walk and my hit. In the CBC half of the sixth, South Side's fielders made a couple of errors. I

was unhappy with the situation. Coach Brigance came
out to talk to me and settle me down. I got even more
upset with the meeting on the mound. I was taken out of
the game, and I threw my glove against the fence. This
was the first time I had ever been pulled from a game. In
six innings, I had given up only one hit, walked two, and
struck out eight. CBC immediately jumped on the SSHS
relief pitcher and scored two runs. Final score: CBC 2–
SSHS 1. Grilli was the winning pitcher, and I the loser.
Guido went on to pitch in the Red Sox organization. He
was the best I ever faced.

After this final game, the scouts decided to see how I
worked out in college and stopped courting him. It was
late in my senior year at SSHS. There were lots of parties, mostly at clubs and beer joints comprised of drinking, fighting, and womanizing. I was becoming the ring
leader. Church and Christian fellowship were a thing of
the past.

Spring, 1957

The last event for SSHS was Senior Prom. Betty Ann and
I double dated with Bernie Brown and Judy Compton.
Bernie and Judy were married after finishing at Memphis
State. Judy became an English professor and Bernie an
attorney. They are still married with three adult children
and several grandchildren.

As was becoming a regular thing, I drank some
whiskey.

Graduation SSHS, May 1957

Another group of Scrappers left this hallowed place. What SSHS has meant to so many people is only realized with the feeling of emptiness after graduation. After graduation from SSHS, I went to work at the Memphis Light, Gas, and Water. I was assigned to the Electric Department as a lineman helper, a.k.a. "grunt." This was a summer job that Memphis State has arranged for me. Two former Scrappers, Gene Harrison and Rusty Brown, gave me a ride to work. Harold Cooper still wouldn't let me have a car. I was pitching and playing outfield for the Coca-Cola Travelers nights and weekends. The Travelers were managed by "Pop" Everett, a legend in Memphis baseball. As the name Travelers implies, we traveled all over the mid-south. We played every small town team within a hundred miles.

I had a good summer winning ten, losing one. In the one loss, the Travelers were playing the Humbolt Allstars in the finals of the Strawberry Festival. Humbolt, Tennessee was the center of a strawberry farming area and each year had a carnival, midway with rides and games, social events, a strawberry queen, and a baseball game. I pitched a two-hitter, struck out fourteen, walked one, and we lost 2–1. Jim Hickman from Henning, Tennessee, who went on to play for the New York Mets, hit two long home runs off me.

A couple of SSHS teammates of mine also played for the Travelers: Billy Atkins and Willie Cross. Dennie Wann, a former Scrapper, also played. Mr. Russo, the Pirate scout, had watched a couple of my games. That was about the time I met a rowdy young fella from north Memphis.

John Bramlett was two years behind me and had attended Humes High School. John and his older brother, Charlie Bramlett, played with the Travelers when they could. They were two tough old boys and soon we were friends.

Other nights were filled with girls and beer, hanging out at drive-in restaurants, beer joints, or night clubs.

"Doing wrong is fun for a fool."

Proverbs 10:23

Mid-August, 1957

I was off to Memphis State preseason football practice. I reported on Saturday, had physicals on Sunday, then hit the field on Monday, running, conditioning, and learning assignments in the morning session. I did conditioning and scrimmaging in the afternoon session. After supper, there were team meetings, caught some sleep, and then did the same thing the next day. School started, football season started, and girls on campus. Okay, this is not so bad. Around the middle of September 1957, I reinjured a knee that I had first hurt in high school.

Later in 1957, Betty Ann Vandaventer and I, along with Billy Terrell and Linda Botto as witnesses, went to Hernando, Mississippi, and got married. My mama and Harold Cooper were very upset. Susan was mad at them because they had screamed at me. There was no peace in the family for some time.

Little Sister Susan

I was seven years old when Susan was born, and she was the first baby I had ever been around. She was so much fun and I loved this baby immediately. As soon as Susan was old enough, she became my shadow. For more than ten years, she had missed only one of my ballgames. She was the best cheerleader a brother could have ever had. This is a funny Susan story. She was my shadow and she thought I could do no wrong. One day she had some fudge. I wanted a piece of the candy, and Susan took off running and said no. I caught her and got some of the candy and rubbed some of it on her face. She ran into the house, hollering, "Joe rubbed dog poop on me!" Well, she had this chocolate on her face, and I was in trouble. She finally told the truth and all was okay.

At basketball and baseball games, her voice could be heard above everyone. Another time, before the 1956 blind game, I was on the field warming up. Crump Stadium was packed, and who should crawl under the rope and come running onto the field? Susan. Not seeing my Susan for several months was the worst part of our family dispute in 1957.

"Every time I think of you, I give thanks to my God."
Philippians 1:3

I wanted to continue in school and athletics at Memphis State, but with an injured knee and a new wife, it became impossible. After leaving school, I caught a few odd jobs:

mailroom at E. L. Bruce Company, stocking groceries at Pic-Pac, and driving new cars off the river barges that hauled them to Memphis. Mr. Ruddle, the coach at A. B. Hill where I went to elementary school, asked me to help him coach. I helped and they won the city championship. Also about this time, Mr. Russo, the Pittsburgh Pirate scout had heard that I was no longer playing football, called and set up a workout for me. I, along with my friend and catcher, and Mr. Ruddle met with Mr. Russo at South Side practice field.

After the workout, Mr. Russo offered me a tryout contract in Pittsburgh. A couple of days later I was on the bus to Pittsburgh. I worked out for the Pirate coaches, showing my pitching abilities and also hitting and fielding, as I had also been doing these as a utility player. When the second day of workouts was over, the coaches and I were pleased with my performance. That evening, two other players and I went out for some beers and fun. We got into a fight over some girls who liked ballplayers. I broke the thumb on my pitching hand and the bone came out of my wrist. The Pittsburgh coaches were disappointed and sent me home. On the bus to Memphis, my dreams of professional baseball were over.

"Wine produces mockers, liquor leads to brawls, whoever is led astray by drink cannot be wise."

Proverbs 20:1

Back in Memphis, I went to see Mr. Jimmy Owens at the Memphis Light, Gas, and Water Division. Mr. Owens was the head of the electrical division. He hired me and assigned me to the same truck I had worked on in the summer of 1957. My thumb healed in time to join the South Memphis independent basketball team. The team was coached by Bill Hill, a friend then and now. "Big Joe" Williams, Don Goad, Joe Bickerstaff, Billy Terrell, and I were some of the players. This group, along with Terrell McNutt, Jim McDonough, and Bill Boyd won the 'C' League City championship two out of the next three years. After the game, some of the guys went to drink some beer.

May 23, 1958

Joseph Michael "Mike" Cooper, Jr., was born. Betty Ann and baby were both healthy. Mom and Mike stayed in the hospital a few days. Mary and Paul Statham, Betty's mom and stepdad, were excited and helpful.

> "Shout joyful praises to God, all the earth!"
>
> Psalms 66:1

Betty finally got tired of my drinking and carousing ways and divorced me about a year later. We tried to reconcile once, but Betty could still not put up with my behavior. Betty had been a wonderful mother and a genuine lady.

Over the years, Mike had been a part of my life. The rides at the Memphis fairgrounds were always good for a Saturday afternoon. We enjoyed trips to the zoo because besides the animals, the zoo also had rides. Overnight stays, school functions, basketball, and holidays were special. Mike was always a big hit with my friends.

"Come, my children, and listen to me. And I will teach you to fear the Lord."

Psalms 35:11

After Michael's birth and the divorce, I was working at a local trucking company. Because of my drinking and other bad habits, I lost my car and everything but a few clothes. The trucking companies went on strike and I was living in a boarding house on Peabody Street and walked to work when there was a day to be made. During this time, some of the South Memphis families who have known me for years gave me help. They included Mr. and Mrs. Fred McNutt (Terrell, Jerry, Ronnie), Doris Hogan (Terry), Mr. Robison (Ralph, Richard), Derlene and Buddy Atkins (Billy, Bobby), Wade and Sue Zarecor (Bob, Sue-Ellen, Glenn). In my own words, "If it weren't for these dear people, I would have starved to death."

"For I was hungry and you fed me. I was thirsty and you gave me drink."

Matthew 25:35

During my stint at MLG&W, some other employees and I would play in the adult touch football league. Rusty Brown, Gene Harrison, Charlie Kirk, and Moon Mullins were some of the players. I was the play caller and passer (quarterback). The MLG&W team won their division and played for the city championship. Some players on the other team were Joe Bell, Tapper Swanton, and Dell Dean. In a great game, the MLG&W team lost. I had passed for approximately thirty touchdowns during the season.

I continued to pitch for the Coca-Cola Travelers until 1961. I realized that I was going nowhere and quit. From 1951 in the Exchange Junior League through South Side High School, semi-pro, and All Memphis, I had won over one hundred games as a pitcher. I had lost about fifteen games and was taken out of only two games that I had started.

I was hired out to Boyd Construction Company and worked on Interstate 55, south of Memphis. Nights were spent at different places drinking beer and meeting girls. Terrell McNutt, Jerry McNutt, and Larry Gately had a band and were playing at different clubs. Cooper, Jim McDonough, John Bramlett (who were now playing football and baseball at Memphis State), went to these clubs to drink and usually get into some trouble. Once we were at a place called the Park Avenue Grill, and I was hustling a girl when three men said something to John and Jim. Before anyone knew what was going on, Bramlett knocked out all three of them. Needless to say, we were barred from the Park Avenue Grill. I did hook up with the girl from the grill later that night.

1961

Carroll Langston, Don Lewis, Al Sanders, and Ray Carter decided to apply for the Memphis Police Department. These guys talked me into applying also. I had no police record, only because no one has complained about me. I applied for the MPD, and then went to see Mr. Red Cavette and Mr. Bill Arterburn at Cavette Sporting Goods store. These two fine men sent recommendations for me to become a police employee. Don Lewis was accepted into the first training class. Langston, Carter, and I were assigned to the second training class. Al Sanders had withdrawn his application, as he had been hired by the Illinois Central Railroad. While waiting to go to the police academy, Langston and I worked on the Mississippi River docks. Jim McDonough and I were renting a duplex on Wellington, so there was some beer drinking and girls most nights. After one such night, we were evicted.   Joe rented a one-room garage apartment on Willett Street.

Langston, Carter, and I started with the Police Academy. Captain Cauley was the school instructor and Lieutenant Jim Bullard was in charge of physical conditioning. These two fellows did a good job of getting us ready for the street.

After graduating from the Academy, I was assigned to Headquarters Patrol Division under Inspector Ed Huddleston, an old school, no-nonsense cop. Rookies were always put with the most experienced patrolmen. I got some good training from George Utley, Dave Moore, Buddy Dallas, and Barry Linville. Lieutenants Peek, Ray, and Burns also took a liking to me. All was going well until I was late for roll call one morning. Inspector Huddleston took me to the morgue at John Gaston Hospital and made me work at the morgue for eight hours. He told me that if I was ever late again, I would work the morgue for a week. I liked riding the ward cars, patrolling the streets, and making the scene of every imaginable situation. I was not late again.

While working the morgue, I saw the autopsy of a person who had died from lung cancer. This person had smoked cigarettes for years. The deceased's lungs were black with nicotine, as was the rest of the chest cavity. I vowed then to never smoke. I was soon permanently assigned to car 24 with Bill Reed and Bob Stratton. Each man had two days off each week, so the only day all three were working was on Saturday. Car 24's territory was the western part of South Memphis, Crump Boulevardd, Mississippi River, city limits on South and Third Street. I soon found out that the police uniform was just an added attraction to the women. I was 6 feet, 1 inch tall, and 195 pounds and also handsome. I was surrounded by more single women than I could handle, but I tried.

Police pay in 1962 was not very good. A rookie made about $300 a month, and after deductions around $250. I had to live in some cheap places. One of those places was a garage apartment on Forest Street—no air conditioning and the floor was linoleum over dirt. Most of the linoleum was gone, which left just dirt. A 1957 Chevrolet was my ride, so with rent and car note, some child support for Mike, there was not much left. Food was not much of a problem as restaurants like Gilly's, Ferguson's, Earl's, Spinosa's, the Green Beetle, and many others fed the police for free. Mr. Louie's at Third and Parkway gave us a discount on groceries and beer. Some liquor stores would sell us a bottle of bourbon for $1. Many of the clubs and taverns either gave me beer for free or at a discount.

The era of what was known as "garage bands" was in full swing. The McNutt boys, Terrell, and Jerry Wayne with Errol Hendrix, Dexter Tutor, Tommy Bauman, Neal Carter, and Bob Dehoney had a group. Richard Robison, Terry Hogan, Bobby Chandler, Neal Poag, and I were patrons at these clubs. There were always plenty of women. Some evenings were spent at Gus's Drive-In, drinking beer, telling lies, and pulling pranks on someone. Willie Cross, David Haffey, and lots of women were also at Gus's.

> "I discovered that God created people to be upright, but they have each turned to follow their own downward path."
>
> Ecclesiastes 7:29

Some Sunday afternoons were spent at Graceland School. Billy Fletcher (the best high school football player I have ever seen), Bobby Chandler, Al Sanders, and I played touch football with a man who is now an international star, Elvis Presley. The same Elvis Presley who, years earlier, came to SSHS and sang on our stage and also performed at halftime of the 1956 Blind Game.

Richard Robison and I were now sharing an apartment. There was a lot of entertainment going on, always. On one holiday weekend, Richard and I threw a two-night party. Beer cans were stacked on top of one another in a double window. Any girl who dropped a can or knocked one over must take off her shorts or jeans. Several girls were running around in their panties. Our friend, Carroll Langston, had been drafted by the Army and sent to Ethiopia. Richard and I wrote and sent him pictures and treasures from these wild nights.

The police department and I were doing okay, as I did my work and got no complaints. Working the election sites on voting day for the political bosses also helped me. Working the three to eleven shift, Bob Stratton and I apprehended a fugitive who had held up a service station and taken a female hostage. The man tried to escape to President's Island, but was cornered by Car 24 and the hostage was released. The robber was cuffed. Bill Reed and I were patrolling in Car 21 off Chelsea Street in North Memphis. A call came in about a grocery store holdup, and Reed and I responded. As we drove to the scene, the dispatcher notified us that two males were responsible; a description of them and the get-away car was broadcast on the police radio. The car was spotted abandoned by Frayser High School. Reed and I doubled back two blocks, parked the squad car, and started searching on foot. Going between houses and through yards, I came up on one robber armed with a handgun. I told the robber to drop his gun and get on the ground. He did. This suspect told Reed and me where his partner was headed. A few minutes later, the second robber was apprehended. Reed and I were rewarded for this work by being treated to dinner with Chief Henry Lux and Inspector Huddleston.

Late one night, a rookie patrolman and I were patrolling when we got a call that a female was about to give birth. On the scene, I, along with the lady sitting in a lawn chair, delivered the baby, wrapped it in clean towels, and made sure it was okay. Soon the ambulance arrived.

One Sunday afternoon, there was a report of a floater (dead body) in the Wolf River off north Second Street. Stratton and I answered the call and found this floater about ten feet from the river bank. I took off my shoes and socks, rolled up my pants, and pulled the man to the shore.

On another occasion, Reed and I were invited by the Jewish synagogue to a dinner. We were being honored for our work protecting the business owners and merchants.

Inspector Huddleston called Car 24 early one afternoon. There was a situation at a local college. A young man and his girlfriend had broken up. The fellow was having emotional problems and causing a disturbance on campus. This young fellow was a large person, probably 6 feet, 3 inches tall, and weighing 230 pounds. The inspector told Reed and me to get this man under control and transport him to City Hospital for evaluation and holding for his parents. It all went down peaceably and the young man was later released to his parents.

The Memphis Police Department, like most, had always used two-man patrol cars. On Saturday, July 4 weekend, 1965, Inspector Huddleston called me at home and told me to be in his office at two o'clock. I reported as instructed. In the inspector's office were Chief Lux, Commissioner Armour, Inspector Huddleston, and Lt. Peek. The Commissioner explained to me that a change in the way patrol cars were manned was being tried, going from two-man cars to one-man cars. I had been chosen to be the patrolman for this experiment. I accepted the challenge. Working that evening from three to eleven, I made several arrests and kept peace in one of Memphis' roughest neighborhoods (police ward). While working with other patrolmen, Bo Wheeler, Joe Hurst, Jimmy Hammers, Buddy Dallas, Gene Bradbury, and others, I was involved in the policing of illegal whiskey, gambling, auto theft, and burglaries.

> "Do not be like a senseless horse or mule that needs a
> bit or bridle to keep it under control."
>
> Psalms 32:9

During my time on the MPD, my personal life and pleasures were drinking, partying, and lots of women. By now, I was completely separated from church and had no Christian fellowship.

Moving On

Richard Robison, Bobby Chandler, Bobby Spinosa, Carroll Langston (now home from Army), and I rented a house at 20 East Holmes Road in Whitehaven, just outside Memphis. This house sat on five acres and Spinosa put his horses in the pasture and barn. The house had big rooms and was perfect for parties and entertaining. Freddie Fredrick was now managing the Rapscallions (a local band made up of my friends: Jerry McNutt, Coon Elder, Errol Hendrix, Tom Bauman, Bobby Ray

Watson, Bob Dehoney, Dexter Tutor, and Neal Carter). Sometimes they set up at 20 E. Holmes and played for the parties. Buddy Davis, John Freeman, Don Hutson, Terry Gwin, Rube Rorie, Frank Spinosa, and others were always there. Girls came from far and wide to attend these parties. Some of them we knew, but there was always a bunch of newies (ones that hadn't been before). It was at one of these parties that I introduced everyone to "The Flame Dance." You roll up two pieces of newspaper into torches and take off all your clothes. The band strikes up a hot song, you light the torches, and come out of the back room, naked with torches lit, gyrating to the music among the partiers. The dance was greeted by squealing, hollering, and laughing. An encore was requested.

> "How could this happen? When I planted you, I chose a vine of the purest stock, the very best. How did you grow into this corrupt wild vine? No amount of soap or lye can make you clean. You are stained with guilt that cannot be washed away. I, the Sovereign Lord, have spoken!"
>
> Jeremiah 2:21-22

I had a friend, Bill Richerson, who operated a lounge on Washington Street in downtown Memphis. The Rapscallions would play on some Saturday nights. The word would be put out several days in advance and the club would be packed. Richerson would charge $5 admission, which would include beer, setups, and money for the band. It was at this club, known as the "W," that the alligator (gator) became famous. The "gator" is done during a fast, upbeat song. On a signal, one of the male dancers falls face down on the floor, then the other males would do the same thing. The males crawled on their bellies toward and around their female partners. Many variations of the gator developed wherever people danced.

The Manhattan, Tiki, Starligh,t and Hi-Hat were other clubs my friends and I frequented. Many of the great musicians of our time played at these clubs. Isaac Hayes, Rufus Thomas, Willie Mitchell, David Porter, Barbara Branch, and several groups that were in town to record at Stax Studio. There were always plenty of fine women at these places, and I would always leave with someone I already knew or maybe someone new.

I had reconnected with my mom and dad during this time. I would mostly go to visit Mama and Susan because no matter how bad my personal life was, I loved them. I made sure that Susan was never out of my life again. Mama Cooper would cook a big meal and have John Bramlett, Billy Fletcher, Richard Robison, and me to eat. Thanks, Mom!

I had two friends, Richard Hughes and Larry Hassell, who were selling cars. Both of these men were making hundreds of dollars more per month than I was on the MPD. Joe Schaeffer, a new and used VW dealer, offered me a job. Mr. Schaeffer gave me a pay package with a guarantee more than the MPD paid, plus commission with insurance and other benefits. With the pay increase and the working hours being better, I resigned from the Memphis Police Department on February 1, 1966. I went to work for Mr. Schaeffer. I had some of the best automobile managers in the business as mentors. Les Ward and Robert Schaeffer were both extremely wise to the car industry. With their help, I soon became an ace salesman.

After working hours, I spent my time as always, drinking, partying, womanizing, and causing myself and others problems. On one sales training trip to the VW training center in New Orleans, two friends, Jack Carasso and Charlie Beale, and I were in a strip joint. I complained about the drinks being watered down. The bouncer and a doorman came over and told me I had to go. As I started to finish my drink, the bouncer grabbed me. The fight began, and Charlie, Jack, and I got away before the police arrived.

There was always something going on at 20 E. Holmes Road and if not there, at one of the local clubs, the Circus Lounge, M and M Lounge, Airways Club, Thunderbird, or the "W." Some of the great bands of this era played at these clubs. Eddie Harrison and the Shortcuts, Flash and the Board of Directors, Tommy Burk and the Counts (Thomas Boggs of Huey's Restaurants, was the drummer), and a fellow who became famous in country pop, Ronnie Milsaps. Billy Hill, another of my friends, had a club called the Nightlighter. Some of the young, up and coming stars who played there were Jerry Lee Lewis, Kris Kristofferson, Kenny Rogers, and Sam the Sham.

For several years, I had made connections with people in many illegal businesses. I had a connection to the drugs known as "bennie's and 'dex," both used for diet control and staying awake long hours, and used with alcohol to reach an unusual buzz. I could hook anyone up with this connection. I knew a doctor in a small country town who did abortions; a business man from San Diego, California, that made porno movies and magazines; and also those who shipped illegal whiskey and cigarettes into Memphis. When Coors beer was not sold in the mid-South area, I was friends with a man who had a small warehouse of this product in mid-town Memphis. I could connect potential buyers and users of these products and services to the suppliers.

"This is what the Lord says, 'Cursed are those who put their trust in mere humans and turn their hearts away from the Lord."

Jeremiah 17:5

In December 1967, I had a terrible auto accident. The doctors in the emergency room said I would not live till morning. I could hear them and in my mind; I vowed to prove them wrong. The next day, Dr. Robert Vincent, Fred Wallace, and Paul Williams worked on me for seven and a half hours putting me back together. I was in the hospital for two months. Once out of the hospital, my friends and I got right back to our foolish behavior. I went back to work at Schaeffer Motors in April. I was the used car sales leader my first month back.

I started dating a young girl, Shirley Davis. She was the sister of Richard Robison's friend, Vivian. The four of us, along with all our partying friends, continued with the same nightlife as always. I was still slipping around with some of my old women acquaintances.

In August 1968, Shirley and I got married. Shirley and her parents, John and Dean Gordon, and sister Vivian, all attended My family, Harold, Marguerite, and Susan were there. Susan's friend, Bob Wilson, was with her. Other family members and friends such as Mr. and Mrs. Dehoney, Russ and Loretta Vollmer, Billy and Marsha Fletcher attended. Richard Robison, Carroll Langston, Bob Dehoney and others stood up with me. After the ceremony was conducted by Mama Cooper's pastor, Dr. Walter Mischke, everyone went to a reception at Whitehaven Country Club. I did not have a preacher as I had not been to church in ten years.

> "For if a man think himself to be something, when he is nothing, he deceiveth himself."
>
> Galatians 6:3

After a short honeymoon, Shirley and I settled into a new apartment. I continued to work at Schaeffer Motors and Shirley went to work at Sears. Socially, our habits didn't change. We were partying, drinking, and I was still hanging out with my friends. The Red Dog Bar, Mardi Gras Lounge, Choctaw Lounge were some of the places we would go to drink after work. Shirley would meet me sometimes. Other activities were family and friend get togethers, and drinking was always involved. Memphis State and Ole Miss football games were attended on some weekends with plenty of partying after the games.

Around Thanksgiving 1968, Shirley found out she is pregnant. Both families were happy and looked forward to a new addition. I made a really nice Christmas bonus and put this money in savings.

I had been talking to Robert Schaeffer, John Jeffcoat, and Harry Jeffries about opening my own car business. The plan was to open a buy-here, pay-here operation, aka "We Tote the Note." I had saved $2,000. My mom and dad, Marguerite and Harold, agreed to loan me $3,000 for ninety days. Joe and Harold go to see Marvin Ballin, attorney to incorporate, Joe Cooper Auto Sales, Inc. Remember, this is 1959, Marvin's fee: $50.

The Coopers had known Marvin and his family from the dry goods store they owned in South Memphis. Mr. Ben Ballin, the boss, had allowed me and many others to charge their clothes and pay on time. Most every South Side athlete owed Mr. Ben at one time or another. Marvin Ballin has gone on to be one of the most successful criminal lawyers in America. He heads the firm Ballin, Ballin, and Fishman. His son, Leslie Ballin, is now a renown defense attorney. In training is Blake Ballin, Leslie's son, and Marvin's grandson. The Ballin Firm has represented the Coopers several times and many of my friends and acquaintances. They all remain good friends today.

The next step was to rent a location. An old night club, The Fire Gables at 2181 South Bellevue, was vacant. I contacted Tommy Land, the owner, and rented the place. On April 1, 1969, Joe Cooper Auto Sales, Inc. opened. Judge Ellis got my license and taxes in order. Lillie Mae Smith stopped and asked me if I needed some help. The next day, Andrew Ellis, Lillie's friend, went to work at Cooper's, and stayed with Cooper Auto for about ten years. I had plenty of places to buy my cars. Trade ins at Schaeffer Motors, Rutland Ford, Daughtit-Carroll Pontiac, and others kept me well supplied. Most business was done on Friday and Saturday when the customers got paid. Terms were $50 down and $10 a week. Business was good from the start. Andrew showed the customers the cars and brought them in the office. I did the paperwork and collected the down payments. By the end of April 1969, Cooper Auto had sold forty-two cars and had thirty-eight weekly notes.

On May 3, 1969, Shirley had some complications with her pregnancy and Mama Cooper took her to Baptist Hospital. I was called and was soon there. Shortly thereafter, the nurse came out to tell me and Mama Cooper that Shirley had delivered twin boys. The bad news was that they were seven month babies and weighed only two pounds two ounces and two pounds seven ounces and had been put on breathing and feeding equipment. The babies were isolated and under constant watch. Shirley was okay except she was worried about the babies. The boys were named John Ryan and Harold Brian. Two days later, John Ryan died. Dr. Gene Whittington and his staff determined that Brian had to build up his lungs. They worked with him and he started to get stronger. Shirley went home. Physically, she was getting well, but she was having emotional problems. I went to visit Brian every day. Brian stayed in Baptist Hospital for two months. When he got up to five pounds, he got to come home.

"The Lord blesses those who ignore him—Those who are fools—Why? We are not worthy, but the Lord has plans that we know nothing about."

Joe Cooper

Bob and Susan's Wedding

"Oh, the joys of those who do not follow the advice of the wicked, or stand around with sinners, or join in with scoffers. But they delight in doing everything the Lord wants; day and night they think about his law. They are like trees planted along the riverbank, bearing fruit each

season without fail. Their leaves never wither, and in all
they do, they prosper."

Psalms 1:1-3

On December 6, 1969, Susan Cooper was married
to Bob Wilson. Bob and Susan met while attending
Southern Methodist University in Dallas, Texas. Bob
was in the Air ROTC at SMU when he asked Susan
to be his flight angel. During and after SMU they were
always together. The wedding was held at Mullins UMC
with a packed sanctuary. Afterwards, a reception at the
Memphis Athletic Club was attended by hundreds of
people from all over the world. This was truly one of the
happiest days of my life. I knew Bob Wilson was a man
of honesty, integrity, and character. Bob had been raised
by Kemmons and Dorothy Wilson to be a Christian. Bob
had not failed them; he was a godly man. I adored Susan
and never doubted that Bob Wilson would be a wonderful husband.

1970

Joe Cooper Auto Sales was growing. Soon sales had increased our weekly notes to one hundred. When I rented
the old Five Gables Club, the bar was left inside. This
bar gave me and my friends, Jim Loosier, John Bramlett,
Hugh Kyle, and others a place to drink whiskey after
work. Jerry McNutt came to work at Cooper Auto. Jerry
was still playing music at night. He and his wife, Cecelia,
were expecting a baby. John Bramlett was now playing
pro football. During the off season he used a car I loaned
him. John and his brother, Charlie, also stopped by for

after-work drinks. McNutt left Cooper Auto and went to work at a large GM dealer. Jerry just recently retired after a successful career in the auto business.

Neal Carter, another member of the Rapscallions, came to work at Cooper Auto. Neal did a good job and stayed with me for several years.

Brian was growing, getting into everything, and a healthy little boy. Many days I took him to work with me. One day Brian and I were rolling a ball in the office, and the ball rolled behind some boxes. Brian reached behind the boxes and pulled out a snake. He was holding the snake and screaming, "Daddy! Daddy!" I finally got the snake, which was just a harmless rat snake. We still laugh about this today.

As Mike Cooper grew older, he would come to Joe Cooper Auto Sales and spend time with me. He was always helping Andrew Ellis work on cars.

Mike came to work at Joe Cooper Auto Sales for a short time after high school. After attending Memphis State University for a while and real estate school sales and appraisal, he sold and appraised real estate. During this time Mike bought and renovated several midtown homes.

When Mike's stepdad, Ed Wright, got sick, Mike took over Mercury Valet, a laundry cleaning business in Memphis. After Ed's death, Mike bought the business and the buildings at Madison and Idlewild streets. Today Mike Cooper still operates Mercury Valet and has real estate investments and other business ventures. Betty Ann, his mom, still comes to the cleaners two or three days a week. Mike and his mom are very close, and she is still a wonderful lady. Mike and I try to have lunch and visit at least once a week. These visits always end with a hug and an "I love you."

Many interesting things happened in the early days of Cooper Auto. One time, Andrew and I were looking for a car because the customer had missed several notes. This car, a 1961 Pontiac, was spotted going in the opposite direction. The repo team rode around the area checking the address on the sales application. The car was found at one of these locations. The tires and wheels had been taken off and the Pontiac was sitting on concrete blocks. I had already collected several hundred dollars off this car because it had been repoed before. Andrew and I took a hammer and axe handle out of their truck and proceeded to knock all the windows, windshield, back glass, head and tail lights into pieces. Raising the hood, the battery was taken out and put in the truck. Then I took his hammer and beat the carburetor into pieces, cut the wiring, and smashed the electrical box. Meanwhile, Andrew beat the car body with the axe handle. The customer who drove the Pontiac and all those at this residence were in shock after watching Andrew and I demolish the car. We got into our truck and left. Not long after that I hired Bob Baker to do the repo work.

Another time a customer named R. Farmer quit paying for the car he had bought on credit from Cooper's. Baker's repo company had picked up the car on Monday. On Friday when it was just about dark, a large truck pulled up in front of Cooper's office. The driver rolled down his window and fired a shotgun blast through the front windows of my office. The shooter was R. Farmer, the repoed customer.

> "But I can't help myself, because it is sin inside me that makes me do these evil things."
>
> Romans 7:17

I bought a piece of property at 2552 S. Bellevue, just four blocks from the original location. When the office and lot were ready, the business was moved. Sales and collections were still good. Soon Bellevue was changed to Elvis Presley Boulevard to honor our hometown star.

Shirley and I were still partying, traveling, and socializing. We never went to church, prayed, or read the Bible. The only time we had been in a church since our wedding was to have Brian christened. I had a new house built in Whitehaven, not far from John and Dean Gordon, Shirley's stepdad and mother. We were now close to many of our friends: McDonoughs, Fletchers, Vollmers, Echols, and others. There was always something going on at one house or the other. In the fall of 1971, Shirley was pregnant again. All went well this time and on May 6, 1972, our daughter Shelley Dean "Deanie" Cooper was born: a beautiful, healthy, happy baby.

> *"Even when the Lord blesses a fool, the fool is too deep in sin to appreciate the blessing."*
>
> *Joe Cooper*

Joe Cooper Auto Sales, Inc.

Deanie was my little princess and soon her mother and I found a church to have her christened. Again after this event, no one went to church again. For the next year or so, Shirley was busy at home and I at work. Some evenings we were at home or out with friends. Several older ladies in the neighborhood babysat Brian and Deanie. Other evenings I went out by himself, sometimes getting in late, usually after having too much to drink. As had always been the case, there were always single women where I hung out.

On a bright, sunny morning Billy Fletcher called me. Billy asked, "Have you heard what happened to Bramlett?" meaning John Bramlett. I said no, but my mind was racing because knowing John, I was automatically thinking something bad. Billy said for me to sit down. He then said that John Bramlett had gotten saved. I said, "Saved from what?" Billy said that he got religion, you know, accepted Jesus. I was in shock. Fletcher then told me to be aware, that Bramlett was coming to see me later that day.

Well, John did show up later. He gave me a New Testament Bible and told me he was going to start a faith ministry. John was different than I had ever known him. There was a peace and glow that he had never shown before. Bramlett knew how I was living and told me that it was Jesus who had changed his life. Bramlett was riding with someone else and said that he needed some help. I asked what it was. He said, "Joe, I need a car. I've got churches and schools and prisons to speak at, but I don't have transportation." I had been riding in a five- or six-year-old Mercury. I gave John the keys, a drive-out tag, and the clear title to this car. Bramlett was overjoyed and grateful. My real motive for giving John the car was for Bramlett to take the car and drive as far away from me as possible, because I did not want to hear about Jesus.

"So now everyone will be humbled and brought low. The Lord cannot simply ignore their sins."

Isaiah 2:9

Several old friends and I were going to TJ's Lounge where Ronnie Milsap was playing. Sometimes Rufus Thomas stopped by for a session. TJ's was a well-run club. Herbie O'Mell and his group were the owners. One evening George Kline, a local radio DJ, and friend of Elvis Presley, stopped by. Kline and I had known each other several years. When I was on the Memphis Police

Department, I would call Kline at the radio station. Kline would play songs for whatever girl I was with that night, calling her name over the air. George was also with me and Fletcher when we played touch football with Elvis. There was always plenty of whiskey to drink and women to party with at TJ's.

John Bramlett had joined Glen Park Baptist Church with his wife, Nancy, and two sons, Andy and Don. Russell and Loretta Vollmer, along with Jim and Barbara McDonough, had also started to attend. Russell and Jim had also been two of my drinking and partying partners.

Spring 1974, on a Saturday around noon, I was working in the backyard and drinking a cold Coors beer. Russell and Jim came out of my house and asked me to come inside. I had an uneasy feeling; I already knew they were going to church with Bramlett. Loretta, Barbara, and Shirley were inside when the guys went in. I asked, "Where is John?" They responded that he was busy with the lay witness mission that was going on at Glen Park Church. My suspicions were confirmed when the Vollmers and McDonoughs invited Shirley and me to church that evening. Supper, singing, and some talking, and Shirley wanted to go, so I said okay. Around six o'clock we arrived at Glen Park Baptist Church where we were greeted by everyone. I knew some of the members at Glen Park from my days as an athlete.

After a good meal we all went to the sanctuary. That weekend Glen Park was having a lay witness mission. This type of service was led by a group of Christian men and women who were not ordained ministers. They were generally from a church some distance from where the meeting was taking place. The goal of the mission was to bring the message of Jesus to Christians and non-Christians. There was some good music, some praying, and a short scriptural reading. Then a man named Bob Roberts, from southern Arkansas, said a few words and explained that we were breaking into small groups. I was put in a group without anyone I knew. This group was led by one of the mission team members. Having been taught Bible stories by my grandmother and mama, also by Mrs. Blanton and Mrs. Crumpler at Parkway Methodist Church, I held my own in the group discussion. The group broke up and everyone returned to the sanctuary. Once in the sanctuary, Bob Roberts gave a short message aimed at sinners. Everything Bob said hit me right between the eyes. I knew I was, and had been, living a rotten life.

My wife and I, with our two children, went to Glen Park the next morning. This was the first time without it being a special occasion that Shirley and I had been to church in years. On April 20, 1974, I accepted the Lord Jesus Christ as my Savior. On April 29, 1974, Shirley and I were baptized at Glen Park Baptist Church.

"Whosoever liveth and believeth in me shall never die. Believest thou this?"

John 11:26

My family and I attended Glen Park for a couple of months. Both my wife and I were missing our former friends, as it seemed that someone from the church was always coming by our home or my office. Both of us decided to change to a church closer to our Whitehaven home. These sudden changes in our lifestyle had caused some mental and emotional strain on both of us.

One evening while at a friend's home, I took my first drink of whiskey in three months. Our family continued to attend Whitehaven Methodist Church, but during the week, we would go out to eat or to someone's home and drink and play poker. I started my old carousing around and "old bad habits."

> "And that which fell among thorns are they, which, when they have heard, go forth, and are choked with cares and riches and pleasures of this life, and bring no fruit to perfection."
>
> Luke 8:14

At Joe Cooper Auto Sales, business was booming. Neal Carter, Andrew Ellis, and I were still working ten to twelve hours a day. There was always plenty of excitement. If a customer was behind in payments or crossed me in any way, I would smack him around and beat him up. On one occasion, I hit a man who had cursed me, and Neal Carter beat the man with a car jack. Another time Andrew had done some repairs on a car. The customer came to pick up his car, but refused to pay the repair bill. When I confronted him, the man cursed and spit on me. I hit him one time on the jaw, knocking him out. When the man woke up, he paid his bill and left. There was always excitement at Cooper Auto.

Through the remainder of 1974 and into 1975, things remained about the same at the Cooper house. Brian had his neighborhood friends. Deanie was walking, talking, and being a happy baby. Christmas 1974 was a big event at the Coopers.

1975

> "For if a man think himself to be something, when he is nothing, he deceiveth himself."
>
> Galatians 6:3

1975 started out about the same way—a big New Year's party. Stayed out all night and was hung over the next day. Cooper Auto was doing well.

Brian turned six years old on May 3, 1975, and Deanie turned three years old on May 6. We had just one big birthday party with cake, cookies, food, cold drinks, and punch. Vivian, Shirley's sister; her husband, Bill Matthews; grandmaws; grandpaws; friends; and lots of kids were all in attendance. There are lots of presents for both of them. After the other children went home and Brian and Deanie went to bed, I brought out the whiskey for those that were still there.

Not long after this, things started to come apart at the Cooper house. There seemed to be some dispute and argument nearly every day between Shirley and me. The fussing eased up as Brian got ready to enter the first grade at Whitehaven Methodist Day School. As Brian left the first day, he was so happy to be in regular school. I watched as Ellen Gerigano, the next door neighbor, drove away with Brian and her children. "Jerry" Gerigano and Ellen were also active at WMDS and wonderful neighbors. I continued to go out drinking with old friends. Shirley developed emotional problems. No one knew this was happening. Around the end of October 1975, Shirley filed for divorce. Within a few days, Shirley and the children had moved into an apartment, and I was left with the house. Brian and Deanie were gone, and I missed my children and just looked forward to seeing them on the weekend. I picked them up on Saturday. We had a fun evening and went to church on Sunday. I continued to get the children on weekends for the next two weeks. When I called on the third week, Shirley told me I couldn't get the children. She said she had talked to her lawyer and some friends and was doing what they advised. This angered me, so I contacted my attorney, Bernie Brown, who worked out visitation. Christmas 1975 was hard on the entire Cooper family. Mike Cooper spent some time with me, along with Brian and Deanie.

1976

The divorce became final. The house was sold. Shirley, Brian, and Deanie moved to a townhouse. I moved to Lake Park Apartments.

"For these people are stubborn rebels who refuse to pay any attention to the Lord's instructions."

Isaiah 30:9

George Tiller stopped by occasionally. Tiller and I had known each other since junior league sports. We talked about sports, other friends, and nights in the bars. George Tiller had many brushes with the law, and most of these incidents had been caused by the associates George kept. He had a reputation as a tough and rowdy man, but I knew that most of this reputation had been made by George defending others. I still say that George Tiller was a good man at heart, but also one of the physically toughest men ever. On one occasion, George brought his son to Cooper Auto and introduced him to me. I felt good about that because I knew George would not introduce his son to many people. Joe, Neal, Chuck, Vic, Bobby, and several others were hanging out at The Place, Club Car, Fred Gang's, and The Cockpit. Sometimes Charles Ivy and I went to Overton Square. Everywhere I went there was always an abundance of lovely ladies. Some were secretaries, bankers, nurses, airline stewardesses, rental agents, hostesses, and waitresses. I had many choices!

Brian and Deanie stayed with me one or two nights a week, and no women were around when I had the children. Mike Cooper graduated from high school in May 1976. Mike and I usually hung out at least one night a week. Shirley's emotional problems had escalated and she was in a relationship with a man named Tommy. This relationship lasted several years, but he was already married. He never divorced his wife, and he finally abandoned Shirley. Today, Shirley lives and works in Panama City, Florida. She never remarried.

Summer of 1976

I took the children to North Carolina on vacation. Brian, Deanie, cousins David, Treasure, and Lisa go to the Land of Oz, Sugar Mountain Park, and trout fishing. We stayed at Grandma's house in Jonas Ridge where Joe had lived. Grandma Tuppy, Mama Marguerite, Howard and Katie Woodie, Libby and John Smith, and Bill and Marie Barrier also were there. Uncle Leonard and Aunt Cozie Barrier who lived about half mile away were always with us. After all that had been going on, that was a wonderful vacation. Neal Carter, Andrew Ellis, and Voyce Norman watched over Joe Cooper Auto Sales. Glenn Barrier, Grandpa Lloyd's younger brother, still lived in the old Barrier family home. This was also about half a mile away. Uncle Glenn (everyone called him this) had never married. Uncle Glenn was now in his seventies, wore overalls every day, and walked with a homemade cane. Glenn had worked all of his life on the family farm, digging shrubbery to be shipped all over the country. In Glenn's younger days, he and several of the locals had made their own corn whiskey, but when I came home, they always went to the county line where I would buy Glenn a case of beer. This was a highlight in Glenn Barrier's life.

Harold Cooper had come on this vacation with the family. He and I had taken Brian, Deanie, and the other children trout fishing and to a water slide. After a couple of weeks, Harold, the children, and I drove back to Memphis. Mama Cooper and Susan stayed at Grandma Tuppy's. I had dropped Harold off at his house and then took Brian and Deanie to Shirley. A few days later I got a call from Wayne Robertson, Harold, and Marguerite's next door neighbor. Harold had a stroke and was rushed to the hospital. I rushed to the hospital where Harold was unconscious. The doctors were running tests and making decisions. Soon the doctors put Harold in the ICU and hooked him up to the respirator and IVs. I called my mother who was still in North Carolina. Bob and Susan Wilson were with Mom and Bob had flown in his personal plane. Bob Wilson got Mom and Susan on the plane and home within hours. Two days later, Harold Cooper passed away. Harold was given a nice Christian funeral and was buried at Forest Hill Cemetery.

I had seen Harold Cooper on many occasions throughout his life; I always showed him respect and never mistreated him. In Harold's last years he would stop by Joe Cooper Auto Sales, Inc. and visit with me. Nothing was ever said about the past.

> "What is causing the quarrels and fights among you? Isn't it the whole army of evil desires at war within you?"
>
> James 4:1

I continued with my bad habits: drinking, fighting, and womanizing. My string of lady friends were eighteen to thirty years old and I was thirty-seven. Sometimes Mike Cooper came by wherever I was hanging out and snare one of the women. Mike was now a fine-looking man himself. In the fall of 1976, Brian was in the second grade at WMDS, and Deanie was in preschool. When I had the children, there was no drinking or "hankie pankie." They usually got a good meal, did their homework, watched TV, got a good bath, and then were off to bed. The next morning we would have breakfast at Pancake Man or Steak and Egg. On some Sundays, we would meet my mom, their grandmother, at Mullins UMC. Grandma, as Brian and Deanie called her, really loved her grandchildren.

Joe supported the school programs, PTA, athletics, etc. I helped with fundraisers, spaghetti suppers, and such. At a PTA function, I saw a lady that I had seen dropping off her daughter for school. I asked another parent who this lady was, and I was told it was Mrs. Weeks. When I was told she was "Mrs." Weeks, I decided not to pursue the matter.

Visits

Old friends were always coming by Joe Cooper Auto Sales. Eroll Hendrix and Terry Gwin came by and we reminisced about our trip to Mexico in 1966. While we were in Nueva Lorado, a girl at one of the boy's town bars got mad at me and a fight started. Gwin and Hendrix both liked to fight. The three of us were having a good time when the Policeo (police) showed up. Errol, Terry, and I were walked down the street to the jail. The chief of the "Policeo," Chief Miguel, was a big Mexican-American man. He told his prisoners to take a seat across from his desk. After a lecture as to what he expected our conduct to be, he turned Gwin and Hendrix loose, but I was told to stay. Chief Miguel informed me that since I started the fight I could stay with him for a while. The Chief and I visited for some time, then Miguel told me to stay out of trouble and released me. Terry Hogan "Hogie" brought up about a time that he, Neal Poag, and I got chased out of a juke joint named "Chams" in Tipton County by a bunch of locals with bats and axe handles.

Brian was playing basketball at WMDS. I saw Mrs. Weeks at one of the games because her daughter was a cheerleader.

Christmas was a good time. I spent time with my mom, and the children received many gifts. Bob and Susan were around much of the time. Everyone went to the Christmas Eve Service at Mullins United Methodist Church.

1977

"The earnings of the godly enhance their lives, but evil people squander their money on sin."

Proverbs 10:16

For the last year or so, I had not been watching over Joe Cooper Auto Sales as I should. Women, booze, and stupid decisions usually made with a hangover, caused the company to lose money. I saw what was happening and turned my attention to getting Cooper Auto back to making a profit. Unknown to me, this task was going to be very, very difficult.

The Cookie Lady

"For I know the plans I have for you", says the Lord. "They are plans for good and not disaster, to give you a future and a hope."

Jeremiah 29:11

In March 1977, I went to WMDS to pick up Brian and Deanie. We went to Krystal's, which was just a few doors down from the school. While the children and I were getting our burgers, a life-changing event occurred.

In every man's life, there are times, moments, happenings, or events that have a monumental effect on the rest of our days.

Joe Cooper

Mrs. Weeks and her daughter came into the Krystal. She introduced herself as Patte Weeks and daughter, Halle. Brian and Halle were in the same second grade classroom at WMDS. The children were ordering food, laughing, and talking. I asked Patte to have a seat with us. When the food was ready, Mrs. Weeks did not have enough money, so I paid for her and Halle's food. Brian said, "Dad, Mrs. Weeks is the cookie lady," meaning the mother who brings cookies to school on birthdays and other occasions. Later, I told Brian's teacher, "If Mrs. Weeks is the cookie lady, I want to enroll in your class."

We stayed and visited at the Krystal for some time. I told Patte that I was divorced, owned Joe Cooper Auto Sales, went to South Side High School, and Memphis State and many other things. Patte said she was separat-

ed from her husband and was getting a divorce. She had
gone to Central High School (SSHS' biggest rival) and
had cheered. Halle was not her only child. She also had
a son, Darren, who had a hearing impairment and was in
a special school for the deaf. I told Patte that I would see
her at school functions and asked her to call me when she
was divorced. We all visited for a few more minutes, then
Halle had to go to dance class.

"God is going to get you!"–Nancy Bramlett

It was not long until Mrs. Weeks called me at Cooper
Auto. Her divorce was final. I asked Patte to have lunch
with me, and we met at a local restaurant for a nice lunch
and visit. Patte went to a school meeting, and I went back
to work. We had agreed on a movie date two evenings
later. I arrived at Patte's house and was greeted by Mrs.
Florence Corzine, Patte's mom. Mrs. Corzine was staying with Halle while we were on our date. Halle did not
say anything to me until Patte started to get into the car.
She then ran out the side door, looked me right in the
face, and screamed, "Creep!" Patte explained that Halle
was upset because I was taking her mama out. Patte and I
went to see the movie, *Rocky,* starring Sylvester Stallone.
After the movie I took Patte home, said good night to
Mrs. Corzine and Halle, and told Patte I would call later. I left and went straight to the Cock Pit Lounge for
drinks and trouble.

Patte and I continued to see each other and we included the younger children, Halle, Brian, Deanie, and

Darren when he was home from school. Later, when I went to North Carolina for a vacation, Brian and Deanie wanted Halle to go. Patte finally agreed and I, with a carload of kids, headed out I-40 to Jonas Ridge, North Carolina.

Upon arrival at Jonas Ridge, Mama Cooper, Grandma Tuppy, and others had fixed a wonderful country supper: green beans, cabbage, mashed potatoes, squash, applesauce, tomatoes, cornbread, and fried chicken. Halle got mad because I made her eat some cornbread and cabbage. She called Patte at home and told her what I had done. Patte told her she needed to learn to eat these things. A few minutes later everyone was screaming and hollering when I pushed them in a tire swing that hung on a thirty-foot rope from an oak tree. Before bed I told the kids a scary story about the Mountain Monster, how he came at night and crawled into bed with little children. They were all squealing and covering their heads with blankets.

> "May our sons flourish in their youth like well-nurtured plants. May our daughters be like graceful pillars, carved to beautify a palace."
>
> Psalms 144:12

Over the next two weeks, I took Halle, Deanie, Brian, cousins David, Treasure, Lisa, Diane, and Tammy on many adventures. Wearing t-shirts advertising Joe Cooper Auto Sales, I took them trout fishing, tubing, to the Land of Oz, to the Tweetsie Railroad, Alpine Slide, and we hiked the Linville Gorge. As the group of us was driving down Beach Mountain from a day at Oz, the radio was telling about the death of Elvis Presley.

Back home after vacation, Brian, Deanie, and Halle started school. Patte and I were dating, but I was still drinking and carousing around. In October 1977, Brian got extremely ill and was admitted to Le Bonheur Children's Hospital. He was diagnosed with a viral condition and was critical for three days. Patte and I were with him almost constantly. The doctors and nurses did a tremendous job and Brian got well. During this time, Brian told me that he wanted to come live with me. When Brian left the hospital, I took him to his apartment. The next day, Dr. Marguerite Cooper, my mom, Brian's grandmother, had them move in with her.

Shirley finally agreed that this was best for Brian and Judge Irvin Strauch signed the papers. On the next school day, I took Brian Cooper to Shady Grove School. What a surprise to find out that the principal was Dorothy Wolfe, my favorite SSHS teacher! Miss Wolfe sent for Brian's grades and necessary paperwork, got him registered, and put him in Mrs. Streulis' classroom. Brian stayed at Shady Grove through the sixth grade. I cleared out the apartment at Lake Park and stored most of my furniture at Bob and Susan's house.

Halle and Deanie

Brian

Mike

Darren

Brian, Halle, and Deanie

Patte's house needed some repairs, so I hired some construction people I knew to get it ready to sell. It was a
nice house and sold quickly. Patte and her children
moved into an apartment in Lynnfield Woods, not far
from Dr. Cooper's house. Halle was enrolled at Ridgeway
Elementary, where she later won the spelling bee and
was the Ridgeway representative in the Mid-South
Bee. Deanie was still living with Shirley and attended
Whitehaven Presbyterian Day School. Deanie came to
visit regularly and shared in the fun with the others. All
the children were involved in activities outside school.
Brian played football, basketball, and baseball. Darren
played football, and Halle and Deanie took dance lessons.
Patte and I took the children to Memphis football games,
Chick baseball, Opryland, Washington, D.C., and many
other places. I still hung out at the Hearth or Fred Gang's

a couple of evenings a week, drinking and fooling around with the local girls.

> "Above all else, guard your heart, for it affects everything you do."
>
> Proverbs 4:23

I took Patte to Las Vegas for a vacation, just for us. I had connections at the Desert Inn, and Patte was treated like royalty. I had a meeting with an associate from San Diego. We had done some business over the years. We saw several shows, Juliet Prowse, Engelbert Humperdink, Tom Jones, Wayne Newton, and several music groups. At a fantastic meal in the Monte Carlo room, the singing piano player sang several tunes to Patte. While in Vegas, Patte told me that she knew about my sneaking around with other women. Then she told me that I had to stop or she was not seeing me anymore. I told Patte that I loved her and wouldn't do these things again. I was faithful to my promise and never was untrue to Patte again. Soon thereafter, Patte and I started searching for a house. We found a new place that was about to be finished. We looked the house over and decided that it would fit our needs. A few days later, I bought the house at 7275 Magnolia Ridge, Germantown, Tennessee.

About this same time, I had been training to run the Memphis Marathon. On December 6, 1981, I ran the race in three hours, forty-five minutes. Susan and Patte were there and saw me at the halfway mark, then at the finish. Patte said every time the ambulance went to pick someone up, Susan would panic, thinking it was me. As I came into sight of the finish line, Dr. Cooper, Brian, Susan, and Patte were all there cheering for me. Also during this time, I was helping coach basketball and baseball for the Mullins UMC Teams.

"Love does no wrong to anyone, so love satisfies all of God's requirements."

Romans 13:10

On September 26, 1982, Patte and I were married in the parlor of our new home. Patte furnished the home beautifully and the house was full of guests. Some in attendance were J.W. and Florence Corzine, Patte's parents; Jimmy and Pat Corzine; Dan; Curtis; and Mike Corzine; Dr. Marguerite Cooper; Bob and Susan Wilson; Michael; Brian; Deanie; Darren; and Halle. Others were John and Nancy Bramlett, Billy and Marsha Fletcher, Fred and Doris Fredrick, Don and Laura Lewis, and many others. Pastor Jerry Wilson of Mullins UMC did the service. Both of us had had previous marriage problems. Not only did we commit to our marriage vows, but in private we told of our love and respect for each other.

I had for over twenty-eight years, from the time I was fifteen years old, been a user of women. This day, I pledged to Patte to never do this to her. This wedding was the beginning of many changes in my life.

"Who can find a virtuous and capable wife? She is worth more than precious rubies. Her husband can trust her,

and she will greatly enrich his life. She will not hinder
him but help him all her life."

Proverbs 31:10-12

Patte took over the running of the home. With two to
four children there always, she was busy. I, who no longer
connected to any of my shady associates, went to work. I
started an automotive battery company, picking up used
batteries all over the Memphis area. High school and college students who needed part-time jobs picked up and
processed the batteries, reconditioned, and charged the
better batteries for resale. It became an immediate success. The auto sales and financing increased, and I built
a new shop.

The Coopers and children went to church, sometimes
even on Wednesday night. Most nights during the week,
Patte had a wonderful meal fixed. No matter what the
mess, she was diligent about cleaning everything. I said
many times that no matter what condition the kitchen
was in at seven, I could eat off the floor the next morning.
Patte was, and is, that efficient!

Brian was playing football for the Little Red Devils;
this was the seventh and eighth grade team that would
go on to Germantown High School. Halle finished junior high at Ridgeway; Deanie was at Whitehaven PDS;
Darren at TSD in Knoxville, Tennessee. Soon everyone
got used to living as a family under one roof. Patte and I
became active in PTA and booster organizations. Socially,
we went out to dinner with Don and Laura Ann Lewis,
Billy and Marsha Fletcher, and Dr. Cooper, usually with

Florence and J.W. Corzine. I was still stopping by my watering holes for a few drinks with old friends. Patte was constantly working at making our house a home and the whole group a real family.

On one weekend visit, Deanie hit a neighbor's mailbox while riding her bicycle. She broke her wrist. Patte, Halle, and Brian got her to the emergency room. The doctor fixed the wrist, and Deanie got everyone's attention. She knew her family loved her. Mike Cooper married Trez Rogers; we all attended the wedding. Darren played football at TSD, and we all went to Knoxville, Tennessee, and Talladega, Alabama, to see him play. Those were fun family weekends.

> "Children are a gift from the Lord; they are a reward from him."
>
> Psalms 127:3

Patte and I took the family on special vacations: Myrtle Beach, South Carolina; a week on the beach; theme parks; water slides; and lots of good food. It was the same another time at Virginia Beach and Washington, DC, visiting the White House and many historic sites. Driving down the eastern seaboard and through the Chesapeake Bay Tunnel, trips to Opryland in Nashville, Tennessee were taken regularly. These were happy family events.

Once, Patte and I took Darren, Brian, Halle, and Deanie to New Orleans. On Saturday, Memphis State University played Tulane University at the Superdome. Sunday afternoon, the New Orleans Saints played the

San Francisco 49ers. During the Saints game, Brian and Darren went to the concession area. The boys were gone some time, and I was wondering if I should go see about them. Suddenly, Halle and Deanie squealed! There they were—the players were flying out of bounds by the Saints' bench. These two small boys were trying to get out of the way. One boy managed to avoid being hit; the other one got run over by a player. We knew immediately that it was Darren and Brian. Halle and Deanie were screaming, "That's our brothers!" The Saints' coaches and trainers checked out Brian, as he was the one who got run over. He was okay, and the boys got to stay on the Saints' bench until halftime. The giant screens hanging from the roof of the Superdome kept showing the play of the boys over and over. Everyone in the dome was cheering for Darren and Brian. When I asked the boys how they got on the sideline, they replied, "We found sideline passes that the TV crew had dropped." These two were always into something.

Halle attended Germantown High School, was an honor student, active in extra activities and also Sigma Kappa Sigma sorority. Halle was very popular, and there was always a group of girls at the Cooper house. On weekends, the girls got Joe's "Little Red Express" truck and cruised Germantown and the surrounding area. Ashley Luckett, Sette Brucker, Celest Pasley, Tammy, Joell, Shannon, and some others were part of the truck brigade.

"Your anger can never make things right in God's
sight."

James 1:20

Even though we worked together making a solid family, there was still one big problem. I was still drinking
beer and whiskey at least two nights a week. Patte called
John Bramlett and told John that I was still drinking
and fighting. Bramlett came to Joe Cooper Auto Sales
and paid me a visit. He told me what his wife, Nancy
Bramlett, had said, "God is going to get you." John and
Nancy Bramlett, Patte Cooper, Dr. Marguerite Cooper,
and Florence Corzine put my drinking problem on prayer
lists all over the world. I had no idea this was being done.
I was still angry for the way things had been when I was
young. I thought the drinking made these memories go
away, but all it did was lead to more problems.

Halle finished at GHS and went on to the University
of Tennessee at Knoxville. Brian finished up a great career at GHS playing football for Coach Jerry Ellis in
the ninth grade and for the legendary Ken Netherland
in the tenth through twelfth grades. Brian Cooper and
his teammates, Vinnie Lewis, David Stegall, Tommy
Ferrari, Dave Bennett, Wray Rogers, Herky Cantu, Andy
Enterline, David Oakley, Jeff White, and others, had a
record of forty wins and four losses. Brian made several
all-star teams, was captain his senior year, and received
the Jacobson trophy.

Deanie tried GHS, but it was not for her. She transferred to All Saints Academy in Vicksburg, Mississippi.

She graduated and went to culinary school in Charleston, South Carolina. Darren was still at TSD and getting a great education. His speech improved as well as his vocabulary. Patte still grieved over him being gone.

On March 27, 1986, I had a grand fortieth birthday party for Patte. Ron and Nancy O'Neil, Langston, Lewises, Fredricks, Fletchers, Krags, and many others attended. Patte was thrilled and got some nice gifts and a special piece of jewelry from me.

Remember "God is going to get you"? Well, within the next few months, I was at The Hearth, a watering hole where a fellow made an unacceptable remark. I knocked him under the bar and hit him several more times. The owners knew me well, so no action was taken. Not long after this incident, I was arrested for DUI. Don Lewis, who is now chief of police, came to the jail and got me out and home. This time, I was embarrassed. After several court appearances, suspended license, and thousands of dollars, attorney Marvin Ballin saved me again. Ballin got the prosecutor to agree to a large fine, court costs, and restricted license for one year. By now, there are millions of Christians all over the world who are praying for Joe Cooper and his alcohol problem.

Saturday, Mother's Day Eve, 1988

Patte and I went to Polo, a restaurant and lounge near our home. After a nice meal, I started drinking. Patte told me she was sick of my behavior and was going home. She took the car and left. After a few more gin and tonics, I went to the restroom. I came out of the restroom and was met by a young man who challenged me. I went crazy, hit the man several times in the face, breaking his nose, then slammed the man's arm on the bar, breaking it. I left Polo and walked home, cleaned up, and went to bed.

"Continue to love each other with true Christian love."
Hebrews 13:1

While I slept, Patte came into the room. As the tears flowed from her beautiful blue eyes, she knelt beside the bed, placed her hands on me, and in the name of Jesus, she begged God to take this alcohol problem away from her husband. The children were all home for Mother's Day, and they could hear their mom crying and praying over me. Even though I knew people were praying for me, it was a long time before I found out what my dear wife had done.

Mother's Day Morning 1988

I awoke, shaved, took a shower, dressed for church, and went downstairs. Everyone else was getting up and ready. The Coopers were meeting Dr. Cooper (Granny as they now call her) at Mullins UMC. I started noticing a strange and unusual feeling within myself. I knew something was happening, but I did not know what. On the way to church, I told Patricia about this. She didn't say a word about the night before. The family had a great day. I still can't explain the inner feelings that I had. That evening before going to bed, I read from my Bible.

Monday, I went to work, still not knowing what was

going on with those new feelings. After a good day at work, I headed on home and didn't stop off at any bar. The next few days, I came straight home from work. On the weekend, Patricia and I went out to dinner. I had not had a drink of alcohol all week. To Patricia's surprise, I ordered iced tea. After dinner, we went home, and I poured out the whiskey I had left there. Sunday, the Coopers went to Mullins UMC with Dr. Cooper. Patricia was just taking all this in and not saying too much. She had seen me try and fail before at not drinking. As Patricia had been doing for years, she was still praying for me.

> "What is faith? It is the confident assurance that what we hope for is going to happen. It is the evidence of things we cannot yet see."
>
> Hebrews 11:1

I was reading my Bible each night and now knew what the strange feelings were. I told Patricia I was through drinking and promised her I would always be sober. Patricia had for ten years put up with my drinking and bad behavior, all the while keeping her faith that the Lord would eventually get me.

The prayers of a faithful wife were answered.

Joe Cooper.

Learning to Pray

Misty Kilpatrick, daughter of Gerald and Peggy Kilpatrick, sister of Gerald Jr. and Jarrett, had a serious auto accident.

Brian Cooper and Jarrett Kilpatrick were teammates and good friends. Gerald Sr. and I were at all their games and becoming good friends. When Brian and I found out about Misty's accident, we rushed to the hospital. Misty was in a coma, and the family was in shock. The intensive care nurses and doctors were not optimistic about her ever waking up or recovering at all. Brian and I stayed for a while. I had never prayed for anyone other than my own family. At Cooper Auto Sales, I read Matthew 7:7, "Keep on asking, and you will be given what you ask for." After reading this, I prayed for Misty to be made well and completely recovered. I also asked for comfort and peace for the Kilpatrick family. I had the feeling of assurance that Misty would recover. I continued to pray for Misty and to visit the hospital regularly. After weeks in the ICU, Misty woke up. The Coopers brought her a copy of "Footprints." Today, Misty is a beautiful woman, married to David Hawkins and mother of Jack.

Fork Union

In August 1988, Brian Cooper enrolled at Fork Union Military Academy in Fork Union. The Academy is a military, Christian, academic-oriented institution. Brian was on a one-year program. Between high school and college, Joe and Brian had visited Fork Union in July 1988. The football coach, John Shuman, had met with them and was excited about having Brian in their program. Brian was the first football player from Germantown to ever play for him.

Surrender: To Give Up

On September 6, 1988, I flew to Richmond and then drove to Fork Union. Brian's football season opened the following day. Brian was operating under the strict rules of the Academy and could only visit with me for one hour. As Brian came out of his barracks, he was dressed in his military uniform. The moment made me very proud. After a long hug, we walked to the inn for some supper and conversation. Afterward, I walked Brian back to his barracks, and we said good night.

For the next two hours, I could not relax; something was troubling me. About ten o'clock, I went outside and started to walk toward the village stores of Fork Union. After about twenty minutes, I turned and walked back toward the campus. As I got to the gates of the Academy, I looked into the clear and bright sky. The moon was full, a billion stars were shining. I started crying; the crying turned to sobbing. I fell to my knees, felt the almighty presence of God saying, "You must surrender."

For several minutes, I knelt there praying, but mostly listening. Still, with tears flowing, I gave up. "I surrender, Lord," came from my lips. I could feel the Holy Spirit telling me to be a bold witness, spread the Good News, help the less fortunate, and take a more active part in the church. I replied, "I will." Before standing, I thanked God and Jesus and said, "I love you."

Christmas, after Joe has surrendered to Jesus. Look at the
glow on Patricia's face.

> "What must I do to be saved? Believe on the Lord Jesus
> Christ and you will be saved."
>
> Acts 16:30-31

There was a new feeling of peace and happiness within me. I went to my room and called Patricia to tell her what had happened. She was overjoyed and started to cry; we both cried. From Mother's Day 1988, I never called my wife Patte again. I speak of her with love and respect and identify her as "Patricia."

Brian went on to a successful year at FUMA; his academics improved and he had an outstanding football season. At graduation, Brian Cooper received the Reserve Officer's Award. He also had offers from Army, Navy, and University of Pennsylvania to continue his scholastic and football future. He chose to give up football and attended The University of Mississippi: Ole Miss.

> "As the scriptures tell us, 'Anyone who believes in Him
> will not be disappointed.'"
>
> Romans 10:11

From 1988 until 1993, things were always on the go at the Cooper's house. Halle finished at UT and spent time in Aspen, Colorado, then went to work as a sales representative. Darren came home from TSD, got a job at the Defense Depot, and got a place to live with two friends. Deanie graduated from All Saints and started to Shelby State Community College. Mike Cooper was busy taking care of his business ventures. Brian came to work at Joe Cooper Auto Sales.

Joe and Patricia Giving Darren his new truck

Patricia developed lower back problems and had six hours of surgery, but recovered in time to spend a week in West Point, New York. While there, she and I saw Brian and his FUMA team play the Army JVs in football, toured the U.S. Military Academy campus, and visited the Culinary Institute of America at Hyde Park, New York, where Patricia talked the master chef into letting us eat a fantastic meal. In Patricia's negotiations, she did tell the chef that I would make a nice donation.

Within a short period of time, Patricia developed intestinal problems. She had two operations to remove large tumors, non-cancerous. During each of these physical problems, the Coopers turned the issues over to the

Lord. Daily devotion, prayer, and Bible study had become a habit with the two of us.

> "May you experience the love of Christ, though it is so great you will never fully understand it. Then you will be filled with the fullness of life and power that comes from God."
>
> Ephesians 3:19

I continued to support the programs at Germantown High School booster clubs and along with friends, Mayor Boyd Arthur, Bill Tubbs, and Ron Tiller, kept the chains at Red Devil football games.

I started to attend the prayer breakfast at Mullins UMC, was appointed to the administrative council, and gave occasional devotionals. I finished reading the Bible from cover to cover for the first time. Patricia had given me a concordance of the Bible, and I used it in my Bible study. Ken Burnett, the minister at Mullins UMC, kept the Coopers active teaching a young adult class, ushering, and having me do the stewardship message from the pulpit. Another time, we had a class for the young children at Mullins UMC. This was a reminder to us of our days in Sunday school.

I became involved with the Calvary Rescue Mission. Calvary Rescue Mission was founded by Milton Hatcher, the hard-living, whiskey-drinking barber. Hatcher owned the barber shop where my friends and I hung out while at South Side High School. Milton had accepted Jesus as his savior and with a new way of life, started Calvary. The

Mission is a place where the homeless and downtrodden can bathe, shave, get clean clothing, good food, and a nice bed. The best feature of the Mission is the evening service, singing, preaching, Bible study, and the plan of salvation. Thousands of men have come to know Jesus at Calvary Mission.

I was elected to the board of directors of Calvary Rescue Mission. Thanksgiving and Christmas were, and are, big occasions at Calvary. 300 to 500 meals are served at Thanksgiving, and 500 to 800 children are treated to gifts, food, and Bible stories at Christmas. While I was on the Calvary Board, Brother Milton Hatcher passed away. After a beautiful Christian funeral, Brother Milton is at home with Jesus.

After some problems choosing a new director, I was chosen as president of the board of directors. With Betty Hatcher, Milton's widow; Rex Moody; me; and others, a decision was made to hire Bob Freudiger. Freudiger, a born again Christian, knows both sides as he had previously lived a sin-filled life.

> "God is so glorious that even the moon and stars scarcely shine compared to him."
>
> Job 25:5

Patricia and I were introduced to Dr. Scott Morris, the founder of the Church Health Center. Dr. Morris, a minister and physician, created a clinic where people on a limited income or a job that doesn't have insurance, can get health care. Hundreds of doctors, nurses, and other medical personnel donate their time to attend to the patients. The more I found out about Dr. Morris, the more I was sure that the doctor was a true man of God. We added the Church Health Center to our charity list. When Dr. Morris came to Mullins UMC presenting the concept of the health center, I was asked by Reverend Burnett to introduce Dr. Morris to the congregation.

"Nana" Patricia and Baby Taylor

John Bramlett was actively preaching about the plan of salvation. I went with John sometimes and gave a brief testimony. Most Thursdays we went to the businessman's lunch at Bellevue Baptist Church where Dr. Adrian Rogers spoke. Bramlett also held a charity golf tournament and a Sweet Jesus Retreat. Patricia and I participated in both.

> "Grandchildren are the crowning glory of the aged; parents are the pride of their children."
>
> Proverbs 17:6

Taylor Christening
Taylor, Brian, and "Papaw" Joe

The Cooper Family

The Corzine Family

Taylor Kaylin Cooper

April 10, 1994, Taylor Kaylin Cooper, a gorgeous baby girl, was born to Tracey and Brian Cooper. Taylor is our first grandchild. She was immediately loved by all. The Coopers and Buddy Wilson, Taylor's other granddad, joined with Dr. Marguerite Cooper, her great grandmother, and all family members in loving her. A few months later, Taylor was christened at Mullins UMC with all the family in attendance. After the service, everyone went to Frank Grisanti's Restaurant for a celebration. Frank has been my friend for years. He played football at CBC against me and the South Side Scrappers. The Grisantis, Frank, Ronnie (also played against me), Frank Jr., and Jud, their sons, operate wonderful family restaurants in Memphis. Taylor stole everyone's heart.

"Whoever pursues Godliness and unfailing love will find life, Godliness, and honor."

Proverbs 21:21

Memaw Brown

Florence Corzine, Patricia's mother, a devout Christian woman, was called Memaw Brown by her grandchildren. Florence got this name because she drove a brown car. Florence had been involved in church, school, scouting, civic service, and poetry—all this while being a wonderful wife to J. W. Corzine and mother to five children. I had noticed the wonderful traits of Mrs. Corzine from my first date with Patricia, and we became close friends. Florence had been a leader in the prayers for my alcohol problem. Mrs. Corzine had suffered several years with Parkinson's disease. On April 1, 1995, she passed away. At her funeral, I told the congregation about how I met Florence and got to know her. I could picture Patricia being like her as the years passed. I said if Patricia was going to turn out like her mother, I knew I wanted her for my wife. Memaw Brown is sorely missed.

April 10, 1995, Taylor was one year old. There was quite a birthday party for her. She was just starting to walk and this was exciting. Soon thereafter, Taylor started calling Patricia "Nana." Today, Taylor still calls her Nana. By the first of 1996, Brian was taking much more responsibility at Joe Cooper Auto Sales.

Heart Attack

In February 1996, Ken Meador, a fine Christian man and the organizer of golf trips, set up a trip to Craft Farms. Arnold Palmer designed this golf resort in Gulf Shores, Alabama. Meador, Dr. Bob Walker, Bill Moss, Jack Wilson, Chris Campbell, John Bramlett, me, and several others made the trip. After thirty-six holes of golf on Saturday, February 25, 1996, we had good meal and went to bed.

During the night, I awoke with nausea and sweating. I washed my face in cold water and soon felt relief. Around six in the morning, Sunday, February 26, , I awakened with terrible chest pains, sweating, and nausea. Bramlett, Campbell, Wilson, and I were sharing a condo. I told Bramlett, "I'm having a heart attack." Bramlett called to the others and told them. Campbell stayed to inform Meador and the rest of the golfers. With Bramlett driving and Wilson watching me, they headed to Foley, Alabama, seven miles away, to the hospital. It was so foggy that John could barely see twenty feet in front of him, but he had his foot to the floor. At the hospital, the attendants rushed me into the ER. John Bramlett explained what was happening and told the lady in charge that we were a group of Christian men and for everyone to pray for me. This lady in charge was a nurse practitioner. Her name is Becky. She immediately told John she was also a Christian and they all prayed. Becky, from that moment on, was known as "Angel Becky."

Seeing Jesus

"For I am not ashamed of this good news about Christ. It is the power of God at work, saving everyone who believes."

Romans 1:16

I was having a massive attack. The team was franticly working to save me and get me stabilized. It was during this time that I had the most wonderful vision imaginable! In the center of the vision was Jesus, wearing a long white robe, with his arms outstretched. Next to Jesus was my great grandmother, Granny Weatherman. She was wearing the apron she always had on. Grandma Tuppy, Florence "Memaw Brown" Corzine, Aunt Cozie, Grandpa Lloyd, Uncle Leonard, Harold Cooper, John Ryan Cooper, and many others were there. The background of the vision was the warmest, most brilliant light surrounded by a fantastic rainbow. I did not get to go into the light. The message I received was, "I still have a lot of things for you to do."

Several hours later, Angel Becky revived me long enough for me to see Patricia and my family. Bob Wilson, my brother-in-law, had loaded the family on one of his airplanes and flown them from Memphis to Foley. Three days later, I was transported to Pensacola, Florida. At Sacred Heart Hospital, open heart surgery was performed. Ten days later, me and Patricia flew home.

Back Home

The bypass surgery had successfully repaired my arteries, but the damage to my heart was extensive. Drs. Ray Allen and Gary Murray worked on adjusting my medication, as my damaged heart was weak, out of rhythm, and causing breathing problems. Soon the doctors had my medication adjusted and recommended that I see Dr. Eric Johnson of the Stern Cardiovascular Group. Dr. Johnson is recognized as an expert in treating heart damage such as mine.

> "Oh, what joy for those whose disobedience is forgiven, whose sins are put out of sight."
>
> Romans 4:7

I was having emotional episodes regarding the vision of Jesus that happened during my heart attack. I was advised by Dr. Johnson to see a psychiatric group, and he set me up with the Chamberlin Clinic. Dr. Daughtery explained to me that I had experienced a near-death occurrence. I had never heard of this type of experience and was surprised at this information. I was given some literature to read and after several visits, came to realize the near-death experience was a revelation and blessing from the Lord.

After many tests and a heart ablation, Dr. Johnson decided I needed a pacemaker. The procedure takes about two hours in the operating room and three days in the hospital. I felt much better and got back involved in telling the Good News, church, and Christian charities.

Brian Cooper was made a substantial partner in Joe Cooper Auto Sales, Inc. The name was changed to Cooper and Son Auto Sales, Inc. Brian took over the complete day-to-day operations.

The Coopers started spending much of the next four winters at the Innisbrook Resort in Palm Harbor, Florida, where we are one of the owners. While there, I remembered what my friends, Jack Wilson and John Bramlett, started calling me a few years ago, "The Reverend." Wilson had suggested the name and Bramlett started calling me "Reverend" all the time. This name was due to the way I had become an outspoken follower of Jesus and would witness anywhere and to anyone.

I, along with Bob Graham, a fine Christian man from Kansas City, started a Bible study group at Innisbrook. I helped the First UMC of Tarpon Springs, Florida build a new family life center and shared the good news of Jesus Christ with the workers, visitors, and other owners.

> "My thoughts are completely different from yours," says the Lord. "and my ways are far beyond anything you could imagine."
>
> Isaiah 55:8

In May 2000, Patricia, Brian, and I were having lunch at the Bol a Pasta, a Grisanti family restaurant. Frank Grisanti Jr., our dear friend, is the managing partner. While eating, I dropped my tea glass and appeared to lose focus for a few seconds. Patricia and Brian were concerned that something serious was happening to me. Patricia pretended to go to the restroom. She called Dr. Johnson's office and was told to bring me in immediately. Several days of tests revealed that I had had a mini-stroke. Dr. Eric Johnson met with us and explained that my heart was getting worse and that I must have a heart transplant. An appointment was made with Dr. Ed Garrett, the renowned transplant specialist, and his staff. Dr. Garrett explained the time frame. I was placed on the local transplant list and would be moved up to the national list as my condition worsened. I was told I could not travel anymore or take on any stressful projects, and I should sell my interest in Innisbrook.

Gerald Kilpatrick heard about what had happened and called me. He asked, "Would you like to join our Christian golf group?" I quickly accepted the offer. This group was formed at Germantown UMC and was known as the Hallelujah Hackers. The Hackers are an awesome group of men, and I soon made many new Christian friends. Around this time, I designed a logo for golf and t-shirts that can be worn as a witness for God without saying a word.

I had hundreds of these shirts produced and gave them to friends, family, strangers, and those to whom I witnessed. I also gaves 150 shirts to the Calvary Rescue Mission and 150 to the Youth at Mullins UMC. Mike Foster, a friend at Pro Golf Discount Store, sold many of the shirts out of his place, and I sent the money to the Church Health Center.

"The Lord says, 'I will guide you along the best pathway
for your life. I will advise you and watch over you.'"

Psalms 32:8

Patricia monitored my every move, keeping up with medications, appointments, and daily condition. Ken Netherland, Germantown High School Coach, spent a lot of time with me. The two of us with Terry Austin and Jerry Ellis, both coaches and friends, played some golf. Sometimes, we played out of town, spending the night and playing two days consecutively. I spent time as a spiritual counselor to Netherland's teams. I told the players about my own experiences and how to avoid the pitfalls of sin and youthful mistakes. I also shared my own acceptance of Jesus and how much more wonderful Christ makes each day.

I spoke at the funeral of Jerry Gunn, a lifelong friend. The chapel was filled with family and friends of Mr. Gunn. In this group were many acquaintances of mine from the automobile business. I started by telling everyone that the most important fact about Jerry and me is that we are both born again Christians. After the funeral, I was contacted by several of the mourners and asked to visit with them, family members, friends, or some group. This gave me many opportunities to witness. From this one talk at Jerry Gunn's funeral, many came to know Jesus as their savior. I continued to speak at any place where the Good News could be told. Patricia and I also went to events, softball, baseball, weddings, baby showers, cheerleading, basketball, football, and anything that young friends were involved in. We wanted these young-sters and their parents to know that older Christians care about them.

In 2002–2003, Coach Terry Austin took his GHS lady softball team to the state playoffs. I was there supporting the girls at every game. Some of these players were Dena Dodson, Stephany Bradshaw, Jessica Harmon, Tori Gast, Natia Shores, Brittany Hayes, and Brittany Miller, also, Katie Martin. Katie's brother, Bo Martin, was a GHS baseball player as was Zach Berry. Patricia and I went to see them play. Keith White, whose grandfather Mr. Charles White Sr., was a good friend of mine, and Walter Andrews, whose grandfather, Dr. Chubby Andrews, had counseled me in my spiritual journey, were two of my football favorites. Erin Calipari and Kelli Gross provided many basketball thrills and Megan Calipari, softball high-lights. Gail Stratton, daughter of Kent and Pam Stratton, was captain of the White Station Spartan cheerleaders. Patrician and I supported her games.

I also witnessed to former classmates and at other gatherings, leading with opening prayers and grace be-fore meals.

"No, O people, the Lord has already told you what is good, and this is what he required: to do what is right, to love mercy, and to walk humbly with your God."

Micah 6:8

Life Long Friends

In 2003, Charlie White, son of Mr. Charles White Sr.,
now deceased, and Mrs. Melba White, took over as head
coach of the Germantown High School football program. Coach Netherland had retired from public schools

and was starting a program at the new St. George's Independent School.

I remained a financial and spiritual supporter at GHS. Brandon Patterson, Jake Kasser, Rashad Cole, Terry Bowman, Zach West, Noe Garrett, and Carlos Dixon with several others led GHS to be 5-A state champions. My son, Darren, and I were there for all the games and what a thrill for all these players, coaches, families, and friends.

By Thanksgiving 2003, I was starting to grow weaker by the day. Christmas and New Year's passed, and by mid January 2004, Patricia had to take me to see Dr. Johnson weekly. On Thursday, June 3, 2004, Dr. Eric Johnson told the Coopers it's time to go for the heart transplant. He explained that I could go ahead and be admitted to Baptist Memorial Hospital. I asked Dr. Johnson if I could wait until Monday, June 7 to be admitted, explaining that I was expected to give the invocation at a SSHS alumni golf tournament on Saturday. Also, Patricia and I had been invited by the South Side High School class of 1959 to be their guests on Saturday night. Dr. Johnson agreed to this, then told me to be prepared to stay until a heart was located.

On Saturday morning, June 5, 2004, I got the opportunity to witness about the Good News of Jesus Christ to over 150 men. Saturday night, Patricia and I shared food and fellowship with the SSHS class of '59. Old friends, Richard and Darlene Robison, Terry and Cynthia Hogan, Tommy and Carolyn Poff, Tommy and Margret Presley, Jack and Nancy Roberts, Bobby Chandler, and Neal Poag were there, and many others including Terrell and Etta McNutt. On Sunday, all the Coopers went to Mullins UMC, then out to lunch. Everyone was getting ready for Monday, June 7, 2004.

> "All praise to the God and Father of our Lord Jesus Christ. He is the source of every mercy and the God who comforts us."
>
> 2 Corinthians 1:3

Transplant – June 27, 2004 *From 1:00 a.m.*

The transplant supervisor reported every few minutes on my condition. Patricia and all those who sent me off to the operating room were gathered in the transplant waiting room. Around daylight, Dr. Ed Garret told Patricia and everyone that the transplant was successful and that I was in recovery. At 7:30 a.m., I returned to room 2939 in the transplant ICU. I was awake enough to recognize Patricia, Halle, Mama Cooper, Brian, Mike, Susan, and Bob. John Bramlett, Carrie Canon, and Rick Hale were also still there. During the next forty-eight hours, while I was asleep, all the medications from the transplant surgery were wearing off. As I slept, many visions of my life came to me, happenings from early years up to the present.

Another Visit

During the heart transplant, apparently when the old heart was removed and the new heart was being attached, I had the near-death experience like the one in 1996. The only difference was that those who had died in the mean-time were added. The new faces were Curtis, Dan, J.W. Corzine, Dorothy and Kemmons Wilson, James Echols, and Sonny Kendrick. Jesus was standing in the middle. Everyone was so happy and peaceful. The beautiful rainbow was over them and the brightest, warmest, most inviting light surrounded them. Again, I was told that I must go back and there was much for me to do.

"But those who wait on the Lord will find new strength. They will fly high on wings like eagles. They will run and not grow weary. They will walk and not faint."

Isaiah 40:31

Recovery

Wednesday morning, June 30, 2004, I was fully awake. My immune system was totally gone, and I was so weak I couldn't lift my arms. Progress was quick. In two days, I was up and walking short distances. Eight more days and I went home. While still in the hospital, J.W. Adams, Earnest Chism, and Terry Austin, along with others and my family, came to sit with me. Shannon Cook, another of Halle's friends, worked at Baptist Memorial Hospital. She checked on me every day. Mama Cooper was there early every morning. Susan and other family members and friends stopped by later. Patricia, Halle, and Brian came in the evening.

My beautiful wife, Patricia

I checked out of the hospital July 9, 2004. Everyone was so thankful for the successful transplant, and Patricia was happy to have me home. I developed some blood clots from the removal of the ICD unit in my chest. Medications cleared this up. Another setback was a case of shingles; more treatments and this was fixed. Gaining strength, I started exercising and working out at the re-hab center.

Many people brought food to the Cooper's. Susan, my sister, had several meals prepared by caterers. Stacey Berry and Billie Coppage cooked and brought food. Shannon Jones fixed meals, and Jan Long brought several dishes. Peggy Whitaker brought cakes. The third Sunday after the transplant, I returned to Mullin's UMC. Dr. Shapard noticed I was coming into the sanctuary and announced my arrival to the congregation. Everyone rose and wel-comed me with a standing ovation.

Soon I was again involved in church, community, and several charities. Supporting the youth and attending their activities was, again, a priority. The coordinators at the transplant kept me checked regularly, and Dr. Edwards did a monthly heart biopsy. I was doing exceptionally well. Before long, I was given the opportunity to visit and council other transplant candidates. I turned these visits into witnessing about Jesus and God's goodness.

> "Jesus replied, my mother and my brothers are all those who hear the message of God and obey it."
>
> Luke 8:21

Mother

My mother is an amazing woman! Even with all the hon-ors and notoriety as an educator, she has always remained a wonderful mother. Dr. Cooper has lived a life of hon-esty, integrity, and love of family and fellow man. She has dedicated years to teaching thousands of youngsters the most advanced sciences. Dr. Cooper is drawing near to the conclusion of a storied career in education. As a mother, she is revered by Joe and Susan, daughter-in-law Patricia, son-in-law Bob, and grandchildren. Dr. Cooper is so loved by her students that for years, they have called her Dr. Mom. I sum up all that can be said: Thank you, Jesus, that you allowed me to be the son of Dr. Marguerite B. Cooper. "I love you, Mom."

> "In all thy ways acknowledge him, and he shall direct thy paths."
>
> Proverbs 3:6

Patricia

In God's plan to get me, it is obvious that the creator of all brought a beautiful Christian lady into my life. The farthest thing in the world at the time from my mind was a Christian woman. Me, being used to having all the women I wanted, was told by Patricia, "You can't act like that with me. I won't stand for it." This shocked me, but it didn't occur to me that the statement by Nancy Bramlett and now echoed by John "Bull" Bramlett, "God is going to get you," was starting to take place.

Patricia Cooper has kept the home, washed clothes, cooked meals, been a loving and supporting mother, and faithful wife. Her compassion for the less fortunate is unbelievable. Patricia has housed, clothed, and fed nephews, nieces, relatives, the homeless, and her childrens' friends.

An article in the Commercial Appeal told of a homeless man living in a cardboard box behind an appliance store. It was freezing outside. Both Patricia and I had known the man before. Patricia insisted that we go get him. We did and brought him home. After a shave, bath, and fresh clothes, she gave him a nice meal. The next day, Patricia found him an efficiency apartment that was furnished, bought him several changes of clothing, food, and paid his rent. The old gentleman died a couple of years later. Patricia spoke at his funeral.

This wonderful lady, with others, led the prayers for me to quit my drinking and bad habits. This was all part of God's plan to get me. Patricia has steadfastly stood by as her children grew into adults. She is the person that Taylor Cooper, granddaughter, depends on most, her "Nana." Patricia has been a loving caregiver as I went through the heart attack, heart transplant, and all the times of recovery. As the years have passed, I have come to realize that the day God put Patricia in my life was the day God said, "I got you."

"Her children stand and bless her. Her husband praises her."

Proverbs 31:28

Forgiveness

"You must make allowance for each other's faults and forgive the person who offends you. Remember, the Lord forgave you, so you must forgive others."

Colossians 3:13

My dad, Harold Cooper, as mentioned earlier, had always been on my mind. As I grew in my relationship with the Lord, it became evident that my unforgiving attitude toward my dad was a stumbling block. I shared this problem with others. Mr. James A. "Bubba" Blackwell, who had served as criminal court clerk for forty years, was one of those. Bubba had known Harold Cooper since 1946. They had served on committees at Parkway Methodist Church, South Side Booster Club, Civic Club, and political organizations. They were members of the Parkway Methodist Men, and Mr. Blackwell had known me since I was seven years old. After listening to this long-time friend, I knew I had to take a closer look at what our relationship had been and start a forgiving process.

Today, I have prayed and forgiven my dad for any misunderstandings and abusive treatment. I have come to realize that Dad spent five years in the Aleutian Islands, isolated and away from family. He came home to a stressful job as an engineer for TVA. Soon a new baby was on the way, and he had a seven-year-old son he had never seen. I think about what all this must have been like for Dad. Why was he so hard on his boy? I believe Dad did these things to make me a better person. After all considerations, and much prayer, I am proud to call Harold Cooper my dad.

As I pray and thank God for all those who have come home to Him, that influenced me in a positive way, my dad, Harold Cooper, is always on the list.

Joe Cooper

"Jesus told them, go into all the world and preach the good news to everyone, everywhere."

Mark 16:15

Having already been an outspoken follower of Christ, I realized that the two near-death visions and the successful transplant are signs that God has a lot more opportunities for me. I, in my prayers, ask God for more opportunities as I now see them as blessings. Every day, God gives me chances to be kind, help, and share Jesus with someone. On several occasions, the scouts have been selling popcorn or cookies outside a business. I always stop and make a contribution. I then get into a conversation with the adult volunteers and the scouts. I always tell them what a great thing they are doing and how that's what Jesus would do. I also share my Boy Scout experiences with them. Inside grocery stores, drug stores, restaurants, and anywhere an occasion arises, I share the Good News of Jesus.

I am a believer of the power of prayer and the study of the Bible. I have read the Bible from cover to cover eight times. Other readings are 1961 edition English version of the New Testament and the Message. Hundreds of people have requested that I pray for various causes and conditions. I always consider these requests to be a blessing from God.

All opportunities to serve and help our fellow man are blessings from the Lord. They are not chores.

Joe Cooper

COMMUNITY NEWS

MY LIFE GERMANTOWN

THE COMMERCIAL APPEAL | FRIDAY, DECEMBER 22, 2006

FOCUS | GOOD NEIGHBOR

Onward, Christian duffers

Seniors for Jesus keeping the faith — and their tee times — all year

By LARRY REA
Special to My Life

For most golfers, time on the course in December is short.

And then there's Joe Cooper and other members of the Germantown Seniors for Jesus golf group.

It's not unusual to find Cooper and some of his friends playing their favorite game year-round, even if it's a little on the cold side. For these guys, golf's more than a game. They don't just take the game

seriously, but also it's at the heart of their Christian walk (or ride, if they're using a golf cart).

That's why Cooper wears a T-shirt, when the weather is warm enough, that reads "I'm third: God — Others — Self."

Joe Cooper

After all, we're talking about a man who had a heart transplant in 2004.

"I've got the heart of a 43-year-old," says Cooper, 67, of Germantown.

We caught Cooper at home only because the weather was "too nasty, and probably too many tomorrow." Otherwise, he'd be playing golf.

"We play anytime when the temperature is 50 or more and it's not raining or too windy," Cooper says.

Depending on the golf course, the Germantown Seniors for Jesus play what Cooper calls "the gentleman's tee (usually white tees)." However, there are some courses where some of the group's older players play from the senior tees.

The Germantown Seniors for Jesus was formed four years ago. Some members had played in a similar group based out of Germantown United Methodist Church, said Cooper, a member of Mullins United Methodist Church, whose mother, Margaret, is 89 and still teaching at Christian Brothers University.

"The golf group is about fellowship and being the witness to what Jesus tells us to do to feed the hungry and cloth them and see to it that they are OK," said Cooper, who had a heart attack in 1996 and didn't

take up golf until he was 48. "The 25th chapter of Matthew wraps it up pretty good. I call myself an old geat. No matter how hard I try I'm still going to be so far from perfect."

All of which is what makes it special group.

Most of them, Cooper says, "come from the same background. All of us were raised in the 1920s, '40s and '50s."

Cooper, who had an automobile dealership for many years on Elvis Presley, started playing golf with the group in 2000.

"I had lived part-time in Florida for four years after the heart attack," he says. "I bought into a golf resort down there and I'd go down there in the winter for four or five months a year."

It was old friend and former golfing partner Gerald Kilpatrick who asked Cooper if he'd like to join a Christian-based group of golfers.

"And I said, 'Yes sir.' So, I joined up," Cooper says. "While I was in the hospital getting my transplant our group had gotten to the point where there were too many people. About 20-25 guys are about all you can handle. They split up while I was in recovery. The ones that went to Germantown Methodist formed their own group."

That's when Cooper's group decided on their new name — Germantown Seniors for Jesus.

"Before we ever tee up the ball we gather in a circle, get prayer requests and one of us will pray for everybody, and then we try to live that way out in the community," says Cooper, whose group of about 12 usually plays on Tuesdays and Thursdays at area courses.

On Thursday rounds, each golfer puts up an extra $1.

"I keep up with the money," says

Cooper, who recorded the second hole-in-one of his career this summer at Cherokee Golf Course in Olive Branch. "Then, we send the money to the Calvary Rescue Mission."

It's not unusual that if the weather is bad on, several of them visit the rescue mission or serve as tutors at Germantown High School.

The group includes Jim Anderson, former superintendent of Shelby County Schools, and Ed Horger of All-American Sporting Goods.

"There is no particular church represented by our group," Cooper says, noting he was joined at the Calvary Rescue Mission by golfers who attend Germantown Presbyterian, St. George's Episcopal and Trinity Baptist. "We're all believers. There's no bad, ugly talk. There's no display for bad sportsmanship. He's (Jesus) got us all."

Sixteen men representing the Germantown Seniors for Jesus defeated the golf team from Germantown United Methodist Church. The group includes (front) James Regal, (second row, from left) Jim Anderson, Bubba Blackwell, Joe Cooper, Pat Whitaker, Alva Dalton, Dean Long, Gerald Kilpatrick, Bill Barcliff and Clyde Regal. Not pictured are Ed Horner, John Robinson, Bud Moore, Walter Overby, Andrew Arthur, Jim Wagner and Ben Stevens.

While I was having the heart transplant, my golf group had grown too large to manage. They split into two groups. When I was able to participate again, the group became the Germantown Seniors for Jesus: GSFJ. This is a wonderful group of men who have sincere Christian wives. All are constantly involved in something to help their fellow man. The Wesley Senior Ministries, Calvary Rescue Mission, Church Health Center, Bubba Blackwell Golf

Tournament for Alzheimer's, Methodist, Presbyterian, Episcopal Tournament for Youth, St. Jude, Le Bonheur, and others. On May 21, 2007, the GSFJ sponsored and directed the first of an annual golf tournament with all proceeds going to the Palmer Home for Children

The mission of Palmer Home for Children is to reflect the hope and love of Christ by providing a stable, long-term, Christ-centered home for children who lack an adequate family structure.

MID-SOUTH ASSETS

Professor, 89, advises staying current in field

Marguerite Cooper
Title: Associate professor, Christian Brothers University

RESUME

Company: Christian Brothers University. Teaches principles of chemistry, natural science seminars, biochemistry and lipids.
Date of birth: Aug. 22, 1917
Hometown: Memphis
Education: Bachelor of arts in chemistry from Woman's College at the University of North Carolina, 1937; master's degree in chemistry from Memphis State University, 1968; Ph.D. in chemistry, Memphis State, 1974.
Personal: Widowed; two children, Susan Wilson and Joe Cooper
Civic involvement: Active in Mullins United Methodist Church, Memphis Astronomical Society, Experimental Aircraft Association

The details

First job: I taught undergraduates as a graduate assistant at Memphis State University. I liked it because I had to learn more than the students knew so I could answer their questions.
Most recent job: Before I came to Christian Brothers in 1977, I taught part-time for a brief period at Shelby State Community College. I worked mainly with firemen and policemen, teaching them the chemistry they needed for some of their work.
Career highlights: The best part of my job is getting letters of appreciation from my students.
Most satisfying career moment: Now, you have to apply for a promotion. When I was promoted from assistant professor to associate professor, I didn't have to do anything. I think they thought I deserved the promotion, but I wasn't so sure I did.
Career advice: Read journals, attend seminars and do everything you can to

stay current. Right now, I'm working very hard to attempt to understand nanotechnology. I'm looking forward to the day when an airplane wing will be made of carbon nanoparticles. It would mean a much lighter plane, conservation of fuel and besides that, I think it would be fun.
Person I most admire: All World War II soldiers.
Hobbies: Reading, spectator sports. I enjoy the Memphis Symphony and live theater around town.
Last book read: "Last Man on the Moon" by Eugene Cernan and Don Davis. I met Cernan at the NASA Center in

Houston. He was the last man on the moon. We asked him all sorts of questions. And he had the answers in an instant, but we wanted to know more.
Favorite film: "The Sound of Music."
Favorite vacation spot: The mountains of North Carolina. I spend the whole summer there with my daughter.
Change I would like to see: A safer world, filled with churches and improved schools. All this goes back to my feeling of total safety before World War II. We had the feeling when the veterans returned home, everything would be perfect. Gradually, it seems we've lost that sense of security.

Dr. Marguerite Cooper has taught at Christian Brothers University since 1977.

Mama

Another surprise blessing came as Darren and I were in the holding area before leaving for New Orleans with the University of Memphis basketball team. With a planeload of fans and players, Coach Calipari welcomed everyone.

In a split second, Coach Cal turned to me and asked, "Joe, do you want to say anything?"

I responded, "Yes, Coach. I would like to pray before

we get on the plane." Coach Cal said, "That would be great."

I prayed for all in attendance and their families, God's grace on all those in special need, and a safe trip. Thank you, Jesus. Amen. The response from the one hundred or more on the trip was tremendous. Why did Coach Calipari ask me if I had anything to say? Answer, it was a God-inspired thing.

Moving

> "The land you have given me is a pleasant land. What a wonderful inheritance!"
>
> Psalms 16:6

In January 2005, Patricia was told about a house for sale. The house at 8778 Poplar Pike is about three miles east of where the Coopers have lived for years, still in Germantown. Patricia met with Louise Jordan, the sales agent. The Coopers went together the next day and looked the place over with Louise. One more inspection, with David McNabb, a renovation contractor, along to estimate cost of many needed repairs and painting, McNabb gave me a quote and contract with his price to make this house like new. We discussed all our opinions. I then made an offer on this house. There was a counter offer. I sign the papers and, within three days, we had bought this place.

Dedication

In June 2005, David McNabb and all the other contractors were finished. June 8–10, the Coopers move in. Shortly after moving in, we, along with many guests, had a Christian dedication of our new home.

> "Give thanks to the God of heaven. His faithful love endures forever."
>
> Psalms 136:26

Dr. Steve Shapard, Mullins UMC, along with Dr. Scott Morris, Church Health Center, did the dedication. The home was presented to God as a place of Christian service. Guests were asked to bring a donation to the CHC instead of gifts. Five hundred dollars was donated.

Update

Just recently, I was presented with an award from Coach Charlie White and the GHS Touchdown Club for many years of support in all areas, including spiritual witness. I was given the opportunity to speak at the banquet following the Heart Association Golf Tournament. This was a blessing as I was able to witness to about 200 men and women.

Tommy Condrey called and asked me to give my testimony to the men's group at Forest Hill Baptist Church. Condrey has been my friend since grade school at A.B. Hill in 1946. Charlie Perkins, Erle Merriman, and Cecil Sowell were some of the men present. This was a true blessing.

> "May you experience the love of Christ, though it is so great you will never fully understand it. Then you will

be filled with the fullness of life and power that comes from God."

Ephesians 3:19

In September of 2005, Joe Tully a.k.a. Josephus, the web-master for the SSHS alumni, asked if I would write an inspirational message every few days. I quickly responded yes. Josephus set it up with the title "Exalt Him." This can be found at www.scrapperalumni.org.

Since September 2006, Cooper has written approximately eighty messages. Each message ends with "Stay on the Jesus Road."

I am no longer a board member of the Calvary Rescue Mission, but Patricia and I support it with financial contributions and prayer.

Taylor has grown to be a bright and beautiful thirteen-year-old. She is our princess.

For anyone who is in need of any organ transplant, I would advise you to give your heart and soul to the Lord, and with much prayer, turn the situation over to Him. It has been two and a half years since my heart transplant. I do about anything I want and much more than most sixty-seven-year-olds.

Bob and Susan Wilson, my brother-in-law and sister, are still married and much in love after thirty-seven years. Both have always maintained a close relationship with me. When we were married, Susan was really happy, especially since she and Patricia had been high school sorority sisters. The Wilsons have always been exceptionally good to Dr. Marguerite Cooper, always including her in many fun activities. Susan always takes her mom to her place in the mountains of North Carolina for summer vacation. Bob and Susan are supportive of many charities and join together with us for some projects. When Patricia called on Susan to help with the prayer chain in stopping my alcohol problem, Susan contacted prayer leaders everywhere. Through all of my heart problems and recovery, Susan has always been her brother's number one cheerleader. Bob and I continue as not just in-laws, but good friends.

In Conclusion

God continually warns us of the consequences of sin. I had the choice of which road to take. I chose a life of alcohol, sex, greed, and other sins. What misery I caused my parents, sister Susan, other family members, friends, and hundreds of others.

After choosing to follow Jesus, I have a life of love, peace, faith, respect, and Christian fellowship with those from all walks of life—an extended family of millions.

My Advice

Early in life, read and study the Holy Bible, follow the instructions God has given us, and most of all, accept his Son–Jesus Christ–as your savior.

Glory be to the Father, to the Son, and to the Holy Spirit.

Stay on the Jesus Road,

- Joe

New logo on shirts created by Joe Cooper.

Monogrammed by Carolyn Hale of Monograms by Cie.,
Memphis, Tennessee.

Susan and Bob Wilson